ISLAND

Pankaj Sekhsaria is a researcher, writer, photographer, campaigner and academic. He has worked extensively in the field of environment and wildlife conservation with a particular focus on the Andaman and Nicobar Islands. His debut novel, *The Last Wave* (HarperCollins, 2014) too was based in the Andamans.

Sekhsaria can be contacted at https://www.facebook.com/pankaj.sekhsaria and https://twitter.com/pankajsekh

Praise for the Book

'In this update of his earlier book on the Andamans, Sekhsaria demonstrates his unwavering commitment to chronicling the life and times of these beautiful but endangered islands. Few environmental journalists in the country have tracked one area so perceptively. This book is a testimony to his dedication.'

—Darryl D'Monte, Chairman Emeritus of the Forum of Environmental Journalists in India (FEJI)

'Pankaj Sekhsaria has been visiting, researching, photographing and writing about the Andaman and Nicobar Islands for decades. With the archipelago facing unprecedented challenges from destructive development, this collection of his articles becomes all the more significant. Anyone who cares about the magical islands and their enticements – the stunning beaches, waters, corals and forests, the unique flora and fauna, and, of course, the utterly fascinating peoples – will find this volume to be both highly readable and exceptionally informative.'

—Madhusree Mukerjee, journalist, author and activist

'Pankaj joined our Andaman and Nicobar Islands Environment Team (ANET) expedition to the remote South Sentinel Island in the late 1990s. We were there to film the wildlife of the island and I have a feeling that it was this trip which started Pankaj's obsession with documenting the ups and downs of environmental matters that affect the wonderful Andaman and Nicobar Islands. This collection of nearly twenty years of his writings tells the sometimes disturbing story of how we are treating our fragile islands.'

—Romulus Whitaker, founder, ANET

ISLANDS IN FLUX

FLUX

The Andaman and Nicobar Story

PANKAJ SEKHSARIA *22 Aug 2017*

Foreword by Bittu Sahgal
Introduction by Harsh Mander

HARPER
LITMUS

First published in India in 2017 by Harper Litmus
An imprint of HarperCollins *Publishers*

Copyright © Pankaj Sekhsaria 2017

P-ISBN: 978-93-5264-398-1
E-ISBN: 978-93-5264-399-8

2 4 6 8 10 9 7 5 3 1

Pankaj Sekhsaria asserts the moral right
to be identified as the author of this work.

HarperCollins *Publishers*
A-75, Sector 57, Noida, Uttar Pradesh 201301, India
1 London Bridge Street, London, SE1 9GF, United Kingdom
Hazelton Lanes, 55 Avenue Road, Suite 2900, Toronto, Ontario M5R 3L2
and 1995 Markham Road, Scarborough, Ontario M1B 5M8, Canada
25 Ryde Road, Pymble, Sydney, NSW 2073, Australia
195 Broadway, New York, NY 10007, USA

Typeset in 10.5/14 Sabon LT Std by
R. Ajith Kumar

Printed and bound at
Thomson Press (India) Ltd.

To my colleagues in Kalpavriksh, whose support and interest has been the foundation on which my work in the islands is based

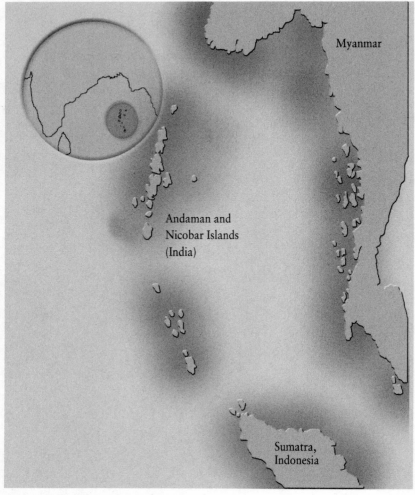

Map 1: The Andaman and Nicobar Islands

CONTENTS

THE JARAWA

ENVIRONMENT, ECOLOGY AND DEVELOPMENT

DECEMBER 2004 AND ITS AFTERMATH

ACADEMIC PAPERS

APPENDICES

LIST OF TABLES, BOXES AND MAPS

List of tables

List of boxes

List of Maps

FOREWORD

NO PLACE IN INDIA even begins to compare with the Andaman and Nicobar archipelago. One moment you are scuba-diving or snorkelling in a coral wonderland and the next you find yourself walking across a narrow strip of silver beach to enter a damp, emerald rainforest complete with birdsong, multicoloured reptiles and insects of all descriptions. Unfortunately, like the mainland, the main threat to these fabled isles today comes from the mismanagement of land and the ever-lurking danger of climate change that threatens to wipe out many islands completely.

Over the years, settlers unthinkingly mined corals and beach sand for construction. They hacked mangroves for fuelwood and to reclaim land. Huge tracts of forests were taken by the timber industry until the Supreme Court of India stepped in. The tsunami caused a disproportionately high loss of human life and property at precisely such places.

Nothing could have actually prevented the killer tsunami that struck on 26 December 2004. The earthquake that caused it was so powerful that GPS readings confirm that some islands have had their geography changed. Trinket was split into three. The southern tip of Great Nicobar was lost permanently to the sea and the land-based lighthouse at Indira Point there is now under water. Grub Island has lost most of its beach and Jolly Buoy now tilts to the south. In many places, however, the loss of life and property would have been dramatically lower had nature not been defied and if human laws had not been so casually broken.

Whenever I have wanted any information on the islands, my 'go to' reference has been Pankaj Sekhsaria who has closely followed the happenings here. His meticulous and consolidated historical record of events reflect his true understanding of the local dynamics. The new articles in *Islands in Flux* provide an update on the developments on the islands over the last decade and also includes most of the articles published in *Troubled Islands*, his 2003 collection of writings on the islands. The articles build on his intuitive understanding of conservation issues unique to this part of the world, particularly the changing nature of tribal communities on account of the disruption of their way of life by mainlanders.

The Andaman and Nicobar Islands have seen upheavals over millions of years that have 'rearranged the furniture' of the natural world time and again. We can only hope that human-induced factors do not push such natural upheavals beyond their ability to survive our inexperienced meddling.

Bittu Sahgal
Editor, *Sanctuary Asia*

PREFACE AND ACKNOWLEDGEMENTS

IT IS NEARLY A decade and a half since the publishing of *Troubled Islands: Writings on the Indigenous Peoples and Environment of the Andaman & Nicobar Islands*, my first 'book' on the islands. Published in 2003, it was a slim volume that put together a set of my journalistic writings and a couple of important documents from the court that were related to the islands. It was, in a sense, a chronicle of events that took place in the islands at the turn of the century. Far from being a complete record of developments, it was still the only consolidated record of its kind and was found to be very relevant. And from the responses I receive from friends and readers even today, it continues to be useful – perhaps as a historical account of all that has happened in these islands in the recent past.

Year 2003, however, was long ago and much has transpired in the rest of the world and in these islands since then. I too have remained actively involved in the islands and have continued to be a chronicler of developments here. I had written in the introductory notes of *Troubled Islands* that the islands have a very limited representation in the national media and that this was a good indicator of the marginality of the islands in the nation's consciousness. Little of the specifics of the local context and local needs is seen or reflected in the national media or in the development planning for the islands which is conceived and directed from far away on mainland India. One can argue that this continues to be the case even today.

December 2004

The islands continue to remain on the margins and many of the challenges – related to the conservation of the fragile ecology, to the rights and changing nature of the tribal communities, tourism development and questions of development planning and policy – are just the same in 2016. At the same time, however, there is no denying that there have been significant changes seen here, nothing larger or more significant than the December 2004 earthquake that occurred off the Sumatra coast and the gigantic tsunami that followed. This brought the spotlight on to the islands like never before and the shift, both literal and figurative, was tectonic.

The earthquake caused a significant shift in the lay of these islands – parts of the Andamans in the north experienced a permanent uplift of up to 1.2 m and islands in the Nicobars experienced, in some cases, a permanent submergence of about 3.5–4.5 m. The damage caused was unprecedented – acres after acres of horticultural and agricultural land lost, buildings and property washed away, casualties of tens of thousands of livestock, and nearly 5,000 people dead or missing. That the islands are located in one of the most seismically active zones of the world was always known. The day of the tsunami, 26 December 2004, hammered in that reality and the vulnerability of the Andaman and Nicobar (A&N) Islands came up centre stage like never before. It was a stark reminder that these islands are unpredictably unstable, that they will always, always be in flux.

What *Islands in Flux* seeks to do in 2017, therefore, is to build upon what *Troubled Islands* offered in 2003 – by presenting a selection of my articles that have been published between 1998 and now. It brings the readers up to date with the developments of the last two decades in the islands. It seeks to lay out the differences, subtleties and complexities of a very fascinating and challenging part of India, a part that is unique and one we know very little about.

A prominent gap

There is one significant caveat, however, that I need to underline. While I might make the claim that this is a substantial compilation on the recent history of the A&N Islands, it is important to note that it is far from a complete record of important developments there. One big gap is related to the Jarawa community, whose interface with the outside world has been one of the main themes of my research and journalism over the last two decades. The recent few years have seen a tectonic shift in the universe of the Jarawa and in their relationship with the state, with the settlers who live around their forests and with the world at large.

It is a change that I am aware of, but one I have not been able to comprehend or investigate in any significant manner. These very vital dynamics of the Andaman Islands are, therefore, not reflected in this collection of writings because I've found myself unable, even incapable, of doing justice to the complexities and fast-changing nature of those trajectories. To fill that gap I've included under Appendix IV, a perceptive and insightful article on the latest developments by Zubair Ahmed, a Port Blair–based researcher and journalist. This is more to convey some sense of what is happening rather than to present a comprehensive account of what I mean by 'tectonic changes in the Jarawa universe'. My gratitude to Zubair for permission to reproduce his article. It is unlikely that anyone has a full sense of these changes, and even as research and writing on and about them continue, it is always going to be a case of us trying to 'catch up' with the Jarawa.

New developments, old relevances

The relevance of a putting together of 'old' writings became evident to me in early 2016, even as I was working on this compilation. The then environment minister Prakash Javadekar was on a visit to the islands when he made promises and raised long-standing issues as if they were new and had never been discussed. His statements revealed a striking ignorance of the recent context and history of the islands, of the various developments that had taken place, and the debates that were already on.

He portrayed the 2002 Supreme Court order (Appendices I and II) as a big impediment in the development of the islands without providing any evidence or justification for the same; he was, in fact, completely incorrect in placing responsibility for a shortage of timber on the Shekhar Singh Commission and on the court's orders. He proposed next that tourism arrivals in the islands should be pushed to thirty lakh from the present three lakh – another idea that betrayed complete lack of knowledge and understanding of the situation in the islands, of the existing infrastructural bottlenecks, of the challenges of providing drinking water here, of the exponentially growing problem of waste disposal and management, not to mention the impacts this could have on the fragile ecology and the vulnerable indigenous communities.

Early 2016 also saw a flurry of proposals for the development of the islands – one from the Ministry of Road Transport, Highways and Shipping for port construction and also for the development of lighthouse tourism, including places that are inside protected areas and tribal reserves. There was another plan outlining development options for the islands that was prepared by the 'Integrated Headquarters of Ministry of Defence' and sent to the A&N administration for consideration and comments by the Niti Aayog. It included, among others, plans for port construction, an integrated tourism complex, construction of a trans-shipment terminal and creation of a Special Economic Zone (SEZ) in areas that are ecologically fragile and also legally protected in the name of the indigenous communities. All this in parallel with huge proposals or ongoing projects for the augmentation and expansion of the military infrastructure there. The scale of what is being proposed in the islands today is unmatched, and its implications for the local people and the local ecology barely understood.

It was frustrating to see that many of these issues had

already been discussed, including in my writings in prominent publications and yet, none of it was reflected in this discourse; the projects were being discussed and proposed as if a new, clean slate had been handed over to a little child who was unaware of a huge world and vast history that existed before him.

At about the same time, there was also a call, this time by Baba Ramdev, to rename the islands after certain icons of a certain political ideology and narrative of the nation. An article that I had written in 2007 (which appears in this collection) was immediately relevant, but had to be resurrected and recirculated to raise points and ask questions that Baba Ramdev is obviously not aware of, and perhaps does not even care about. It became clear that even if something may have been written more than a decade ago, it remained relevant. In some senses it was more relevant than before and it was important that those stories and points of view be dusted out, be given some traction and be sent out again into circulation and discussion. In this, *Islands in Flux* shares the same agenda as that of *Troubled Islands*, and if this helps make even a marginal difference, I would believe it has been worth the effort.

My gratitude

There are many individuals and institutions that I need to thank for being part of my now two-decade long journey in the islands. Firstly, I would like to thank all my colleagues at Kalpavriksh, a remarkable organization that I am distinctly lucky to be part of. My gratitude also to the Bombay Natural History Society, Madras Crocodile Bank Trust, Andaman and Nicobar Islands Environment Team, and the Human Rights Law Network for their support and collaboration at different points of time and on different issues. I would like in particular to thank Samir Acharya and his organization, the Society for Andaman and Nicobar Ecology (SANE), that has led the campaign on tribal rights and the environment in the islands ever since I started working there.

My sincere thanks also to the various publications where articles in this compilation first appeared – namely, the *Frontline, The Hindu, Sanctuary Asia, Tehelka, Down to Earth,* the *Times of India, Inter Press Service, Economic and Political Weekly* and *Indian Birds.* What appears in *Islands in Flux* is primarily reprints of the originals as they were published, with only some nominal editing changes to remove inconsistencies and repetitions. Footnotes have also been introduced in some places either to offer clarifications, to provide a context or, where relevant, an update on the latest situation. I am grateful to these and the other publications that have, over the years, given me space to write.

Many thanks to Bittu Sahgal for the Foreword and to Harsh Mander for the Introduction to the book, to my publishers HarperCollins India and my editors, Ajitha G.S. and Antony Thomas, for agreeing to publish *Islands in Flux,* and in helping me keep the islands in focus!

INTRODUCTION:
CONTESTED IMAGINATIONS

Harsh Mander

THE IDYLLIC ISLANDS IN the Bay of Bengal and the Andaman Sea – the 500-odd-island archipelago of the Andaman and Nicobar Islands stretching from the south of Myanmar to the north of Sumatra in Indonesia – are today at an emblematic crossroads. The many predicaments of this island chain represent some of the classic dilemmas of modernization and of contested notions of development.

Pankaj Sekhsaria, scholar, journalist, environmentalist and occasional novelist, has developed a close kinship with the islands, and has written insightfully and sensitively about its environment and people for over two decades. This updated collection of his many writings as a chronicler of the islands are a welcome and valuable resource to those who seek to make sense of the many contestations that surround these islands.

The modernist imagination of the current Central

government for the islands include, according to the recent statement of Union minister Prakash Javadekar, a tenfold increase in tourist traffic to the islands, from the current three lakh annual arrivals to thirty lakhs, relaxation in environmental and coastal protection norms for tourism and other economic activities, jetty and port development and greater thrust to military infrastructure in the islands. This imagination is impatient with concerns about the impact all of this would have on the environment and indigenous populations of the islands, and regard these as antiquated and dogmatic impediments to the healthy economic growth of the islands. Sekhsaria's painstakingly researched and argued articles attempt to answer these critiques.

Sekhsaria reminds us that the original residents of the islands – the Great Andamanese, the Onge, the Jarawa and the Sentinelese – have a history that dates back at least 40,000 years. For perspective and a context, he says, if the real history of the islands is ever written, the British would be no more than a page and India could be only a paragraph. Yet in just the last 150 years, their population has been reduced from 5,000 to just 500, and today even these numbers are gravely threatened. The Great Andamanese have been reduced to only about fifty, and the Onge a little more than a hundred.

He points, for instance, to the predicament of the Onge, who in the 1960s were the sole inhabitants of Little Andaman. Today, there are 120 outsiders for every Onge in the island, and their numbers are growing. This forced contact has rendered the Onge vulnerable to illness, and exposed them to alcohol addiction and sexual exploitation. The local administration introduced them to foodstuffs like rice, lentils and biscuits, whereas their traditional food was the meat of boars and turtles, fish, tubers and honey. Houses with asbestos roofs, unsuited to the climate were built for them in their settlements. A cash economy was introduced in a community that did not even have a barter system, and cattle-rearing for a people who did not consume milk.

Part of the modernist agenda brought in by colonial rulers and continued in the first half-century after Independence, Sekhsaria tells us, was of logging timber from the rich forests of the islands. In the last century, 9–13 per cent of the forests have been clear-felled, and a much larger proportion has been degraded. Plywood mills were incentivized by high subsidies. In parts of the coast along Little Andaman Island, live coral was reduced to just 11 per cent because of soil erosion due to logging, and the saltwater crocodile and wild pig were threatened. Those who have suffered most, he reminds us, are the indigenous people for whom forests are home.

In 2002, the Supreme Court ordered a substantial reduction in commercial forestry, a ban on timber transport to anywhere in the country, preventing further in-migration from the Indian mainland, stopping sand mining, and the closure of the Andaman Trunk Road (ATR) passing through the Jarawa Tribal Reserve. But Sekhsaria documents the violation of several of these orders by the administration. Sand mining continues to feed the insatiable construction boom of Port Blair, destroying turtle-nesting sites; the influx of people from mainland India continues unabated; and perhaps most flagrantly, the ATR remains open even up to the present day.

The consequences of failing to close the ATR, as Sekhsaria points out, have been very damaging to the Jarawa. These include a measles outbreak in 1999, introduction of alcohol and tobacco among the Jarawa leading to addictions and sexual exploitation, and the influx of tourists who exoticized the Jarawa and sought to catch sight of them naked. Nothing happened even after the international outrage when a video showing naked Jarawa women dancing for tourists surfaced in 2012, and the Jarawa still remain exposed to exploitation by poachers and settlers. Sekhsaria points to the mindset of the local administration, describing the areas they inhabit as being Jarawa-infested!

Sekhsaria describes the immediate and permanent impacts of the 2004 tsunami, altering and damaging the environment of the islands permanently. But the greater dangers emanate, as Sekhsaria reminds us, from the developmental and militaristic imaginations of the administration for the fragile and ancient islands. He refers to the then president A.P.J. Abdul Kalam's vision for the islands during his visit in 2004 after the tsunami. He wanted the islands to receive a million tourists annually, together with deep-sea fishing, bamboo exploitation and value-added coconut products. But Sekhsaria points to the enormous problems of the islands even at present to provide water, food, infrastructure and housing sustainably to its populations. He adds that the island chain is a fragile biodiversity hot spot that is home to a number of very vulnerable ancient peoples. 'Suggesting that one million people should be allowed here is an open invitation for disaster.'

He describes with equal alarm the strategic defence and security imaginations for the islands. Analyst Ashok Malik in 2014 described the islands as a 'prized piece of mid-ocean real estate'. In 2009, Kalam, who had by then retired, proposed for the islands, among other things, a 250 MW nuclear power plant, bases for static aircraft carrier with dynamic warfare systems, and a nuclear submarine-based fleet. It is not a coincidence that Kalam has acquired an almost folk-hero status for India's middle class, and that his imaginations for the islands, as much as for India, were essentially both militaristic and based on the hegemonic market-growth model, with little patience for questions of sustainability and equity.

Sekhsaria's collection of elegantly written essays over two decades of his engagement with the islands are a valuable guide to understand the challenges of one of the most exquisitely beautiful and gravely threatened parts of India. But even more importantly, he points urgently and passionately to larger questions, about the competing imaginations of development, of the ethical and political challenges for finding ways that jobs and wealth can be produced without destroying what nature has built over millennia, and our responsibility to ancient peoples, barely a few hundred in numbers, to let them live with safety, dignity, agency and real choices in our world that has no time or value for them and the environment that has been theirs for 40,000 years.

THE ANDAMAN AND NICOBAR ISLANDS: A PROFILE

THE ANDAMAN AND NICOBAR Islands are the largest archipelago system in the Bay of Bengal, consisting of about 306 islands and 206 rocks and rocky outcrops, and covering a total area of about 8,200 sq. km. Only thirty-eight of these islands are inhabited; of these, eleven are in the Andaman group and thirteen in the Nicobars. This large archipelago is separated from mainland India by about 1,200 km. The nearest land mass in the north is Myanmar, roughly 280 km from Landfall Island, the northernmost island in the group. The closest land mass to Great Nicobar in the south is Sumatra, located at a distance of 145 km.

The islands of the archipelago lie in a crescent that stretches from Cape Negrais of Myanmar to the Banda Arc of Sumatra (Indonesia). The Andamans are considered to be the extensions of the submerged Arakan Yoma mountain range of Myanmar, while the Mentawei Island to the south and south-west of Sumatra are presumed to be a southern continuation of the Nicobars.

The Great Andaman group of islands is made up of the North, Middle and South Andaman Islands, with Baratang Island situated between the Middle and the South Andaman Islands. Ritchie's Archipelago is a group of islands to the east of the Middle Andaman while the Labyrinth group of islands is situated south-west of South Andaman. Ninety per cent of the total land area of 6,408 sq. km of the Andaman group is constituted of reserve forests and protected areas. Of this land, 36 per cent is designated as tribal reserve. Narcondam and Barren Islands are two islands here which are of volcanic origin. The former is an extinct volcano, while the latter is still active.

The Nicobar group is spread over an area of 1,841 sq. km, of which 1,542 are forests. The Nicobars are separated from the Andamans by the Ten Degree Channel, a wide gap of 160 km. This group consists of twenty-four islands in three distinct clusters. The northern group consists of Car Nicobar and Battimalv; the central or the Nancowry group consists of Tillangchong, Chaura, Terasa, Bompoka, Trinket, Camorta, Katchal and Nancowry; the southern group consists of the two large islands of Little and Great Nicobar together with Pigeon, Megapode, Kondul, Pilo Milo, Menchal, Treis, Trak and Meroe Islands. The entire Nicobars has been declared a tribal reserve.

The islands are situated in the equatorial belt, are exposed to marine influences and have a tropical climate that is warm, humid and equitable. The temperature ranges from 18 degree C to 35 degree C and the islands receive rains from both the north-east and the south-west monsoons. Average annual rainfall ranges from 3,000 to 3,500 mm and humidity varies from 66 to 85 per cent.

SETTING THE CONTEXT

1

A HISTORY OF ALIENATION

The Hindu Folio, 16 July 2000

THE HISTORY OF THE Andaman and Nicobar Islands is today a conveniently comfortable one: of the British, Kalapani and the Cellular Jail, of World War I and the Japanese occupation, of Netaji Subhas Chandra Bose, Veer Savarkar, the first hoisting of the Indian national flag, and of a modern mini India where all communities and religions live in peace and harmony.

But like all histories, this one too is incomplete. It is the story of the victors, of the people who have today come to dominate these islands. The vanquished, as they say, have no tales to tell. The history of these islands as we tell it, as we are told it is, is silent in many parts. There are gaping holes that are conveniently allowed to remain as they are.

This history says nothing of the past, the present and the future of those people and communities that originally belong to the islands. For that matter, the islands belong to them, but ironically, the people who write the history are we, the citizens of the modern democratic Indian state. The people in question are the ancient tribal communities that live here in the Andaman Islands – the Great Andamanese, the Onge, the Jarawa and the Sentinelese. These are communities that have lived and flourished here for at least 40,000 years, but the end could well be round the corner. Just 150 years ago, the population of these tribal communities was estimated to be at least 5,000. Today, however, while the total population of the Andaman and Nicobar Islands has risen to about 0.4 million, the population of these four communities put together is not more than a mere 500.[1]

These communities of thousands of individuals with a living lineage going back thousands of years have been brought to this sorry state in a mere 150 years. It definitely began with the British and their policies, which have been kept up with clinical efficiency by modern, independent India.

Independent India was only about a couple of decades old, a young thriving democracy as it would have been called then. But this vibrant democracy was already on course to becoming a colonizer itself. From a colony of the British to the colonizer of the Andaman Islands (and many other places too), the transition for India was an amazingly easy one; almost, it would seem, a natural one. In the late 1960s, an official plan of the Government of India to 'colonize' (and this was the term used) the Andaman and Nicobar Islands was firmly in place.

The forests were 'wastelands' that needed to be tamed, settled and developed. It did not matter that these forests

---

[1] See Tables 3 and 4 (in Chapter 8) for official census figures.

were the home of myriad plants and animals that had evolved over aeons. It did not matter that ancient tribal peoples were living here for centuries, neither that they were physically and spiritually sustained by these forests. The idea that forests could mean more than just the timber the trees provided had not even taken seed in the national consciousness. The Nehruvian dream of massive industrialization was calling and the rich evergreen forests of the islands promised abundant timber to fuel it. The tribals too had to be civilized, brought into the Indian mainstream. There was no question of inquiring, let alone trying to understand and factor in, what it was that the Onge, the Andamanese or the Jarawa themselves wanted.

Tribal cultures the world over are intricately linked with the forests they live in. The story, or should we call it the 'history' of modern civilization, is largely one of the taming and destroying the great forests of the world and the innumerable tribal communities that lived therein. The Andaman Islands is a good example. By various means, both intended and unintended, the tribal communities have been constantly alienated from their forests, their lands and their very cosmos that is built around all these.

One of the subtle but classic examples is the Hinduization of the name Andaman itself and the attempt to pass it off as the only truth. The standard and universal answer to the question of the origin of the name is the well-known Hindu god Hanuman. That the state too conveniently believes this is evident from the fact this is the story that goes out in the sound-and-light show that plays every evening at the Cellular Jail in Port Blair. No one is bothered that there are many other explanations as to why the Andamans are called so. *Researches on Ptolemy's Geography of Eastern Asia*, a book written by Colonel G.F. Gerini in 1909, makes incredible reading in this context, but obviously, not many have bothered to read it. It is hardly surprising then that we care even less to know what the tribals themselves call these islands.

The repercussions of this dominant mindset are all too evident when one looks at what is happening to the forests and the tribal communities. The Great Andamanese have been wiped out as a viable community: only about fifty members of that community survive today. The Onges of the island of Little Andaman (they call it Egu-belong) today number only 100. The 1901 census estimated their population to be 601.

Till a couple of years ago, the Jarawas were extremely hostile to the outside world. This hostility and self-maintained isolation in the impenetrable rainforests of these islands had ensured that their community, culture and forest home remained intact and unharmed. But it was never our intention to let them be. The Andaman Trunk Road was constructed through the heart of the very forests the Jarawas call home. It destroyed precious forests and brought in various developments that are proving to be disastrous for the Jarawas. As a result of a combination of such factors, most not known or understood, the Jarawas recently shed their hostility and have begun to come out from their forests 'voluntarily' (Chapter 8). It could well be the first step on the route that the Great Andamanese and the Onge were forced to take many decades ago. A huge epidemic of measles hit the Jarawas in 1999 and a number of them were, reportedly, affected by other ailments too (see Chapters 8 and 9).

The lessons of history have not been learnt. Maybe they are being deliberately ignored. It could well be worth our while to get these tribals out of our way. Only then can the precious tropical hardwoods that are found in their forests and the very lands that these forests stand on be put to 'productive' use. Little Andaman is a classic case. In the 1960s and '70s, thousands of settlers from mainland India were brought in and settled here. The forests too were opened up for logging in the early 1970s as part of the 'colonization' plan. An Onge tribal reserve was created, but for more than a decade now this reserve has been violated for timber extraction. The attitude of the settlers who today live on the land that belongs to the Onge only reflects that of the powers that be. They ridicule the tribals as uncivilized junglees. Vices like alcoholism were introduced; the addiction is now used by the settlers to exploit resources from the forests. Poaching and encroachment inside the Onge reserve too are ever on the increase.

In the early 1960s, the Onge were the sole inhabitants of Little Andaman. Today, for each Onge, there are at least 120 outsiders here, and this imbalance is rapidly increasing. What more needs to be said?

2

A BRIEF HISTORY OF LOGGING

Economic and Political Weekly,
21 September 2001[1]

THE MAIN TIMBER OPERATIONS in these islands are limited to the Andaman Islands only. Though there has been deforestation in the Nicobars for the establishment of settlements, the timber industry has so far stayed away from operating there.

Like in the rest of India, the prime responsibility for starting the forestry in these islands too rests with the British. In fact, the British were the first outsiders who were able to successfully establish their settlements on the islands. It was in 1789 that Lieutenant Archibald Blair of the British Indian Navy was appointed to survey the islands with a view to finding a harbour, ' ... where fleets in the time of

---

[1] 'A brief history of logging' is an extract from a larger paper 'Deforestation in Andaman and Nicobar: Its impact on Onge', published in the *Economic and Political Weekly*, 21 September 2001.

war can refit by any means ... or to which any part or the whole may retire in the event of a disastrous conflict with the enemy'. A small settlement was set up in the island of North Andaman. However, this proved disastrous due to the prevalence of various diseases, particularly malaria, and the attempt was abandoned pretty soon. Attempts were made again by the British in the late 1850s and they were able to establish Port Blair as a penal settlement in 1858, mainly for criminals from mainland India and later for freedom fighters too. Large tracts of land were first cleared in 1858 for the penal settlement itself. By 1870, the limited exploitation of hardwoods had already begun here. The forest department, with the responsibility of timber extraction, was started in 1883. The Chatham Saw Mill was set up around this time and was for a long time considered the biggest sawmill in the whole of Asia. It is operational even today.

The 1901 census report of the islands, for the first time, lists forestry as a source of employment and also lists about 900 individuals involved in various activities like extraction, sawmills and firewood. According to the then chief commissioner of the islands, Lt Colonel Sir Richard C. Temple, '... this is a comparatively new department for utilizing convict labour and is now the chief source of revenue in cash' (Census of India 1901). In 1929, the Swedish Match Company, later renamed Western India Match Company (WIMCO), started a match splint factory in Port Blair. This remained the only private forest-based industry here till the early 1960s, when the plywood mills were first set up.

With India gaining independence from the British in 1947, a new phase began for the islands too. A colonial hangover was evident in independent India's 'colonization scheme' for the islands, as a part of which thousands of people were brought from mainland India and settled here. What has also been important is the strategic location of the island chain in the Bay of Bengal, close to countries in South-East Asia and just north of an important commercial shipping lane. One strategy of the Government of India to maintain its advantage and strengthen claim over the islands has been to encourage more and more mainlanders to come and settle here.

These two factors have been largely responsible for the population growth witnessed in the last few decades, starting in the 1950s (Table 3, Chapter 8). As a matter of fact, in the early years, various incentives were offered to people to come and settle here. Each settler household was given around 1.6 hectares (ha) of flat land for paddy, around 2 ha of hilly land for tree crops, and around 2.5 ha to build a homestead. Twelve tonnes of royalty-free timber were given for house construction and an additional five tonnes for house repairs every five years.

The growth in population meant that the pressures on the forest – both direct and indirect – also increased. It is clear that the growth in the timber extraction operations corresponds directly to the growth in the population of the islands. This destruction of the forests for the extraction of timber was in addition to the clear-felling that was done for the settlements themselves (Table 2). It has been estimated that between 9 and 13 per cent of the total land area of the islands has been clear-felled in little more than a century of operations. There is no consensus on the actual area that still remains under forest cover and some observers are of the opinion that a large part of this forest is degraded and under secondary growth.

With the growing population of migrants on the islands, there was a need for the government to create employment opportunities for the people. The abundant forests and the timber they offered became the obvious source for generation of both income and employment. The British had already started operations, but their expansion had been limited. Till the 1960s, the Chatham Saw Mill and the WIMCO match splint factory were the only major timber units in the islands. However, the growing influx of people here meant that the industry would have to expand.

In the initial years following Independence, the administration offered huge incentives to industry in the form of subsidies (Table 1), to make it attractive for an entrepreneur to invest here. These were largely made use of by the private plywood industry that began in the late 1950s and has continued till date.

Today, the timber-based industry in the Andamans comprises two government sawmills, some small private sawmills and furniture-making units and three private plywood units. It is these private plywood mills that are the largest consumers of the timber in the islands today, their intake accounting for roughly 70 per cent of the 75,000 cu. m of timber logged here annually.[2]

What is most significant is that nearly 98 per cent of

---

[2] The timber industries and timber extraction operations mentioned here stopped operations following commercial difficulties and Supreme Court orders of October 2001 and May 2002. These are discussed in detail in Chapters 4, 5 and 6; also in Appendices 1 and 2). Some limited logging was allowed eventually, exclusively for local use and to meet local demands. The plywood mills have, however, stopped operation completely.

Table 1: Transport subsidy paid to industry for import and export of goods to and from the islands to mainland India (in Rs lakh)

Year	Medium-Scale Wood-Based Industries		Small-Scale Wood-Based Industries		Other Industries		Total
	Import	Export	Import	Export	Import	Export	
1991-92	29.14	129.50	00	44.35	5.58	0.00	208.57
1992-93	57.25	71.74	00	51.52	5.72	0.00	186.23
1993-94	43.57	107.01	00	38.22	2.29	0.00	191.09
1994-95	95.10	300.30	00	171.60	5.01	0.00	572.01
1995-96	00.00	00.00	00	00.00	1.28	0.00	1.28
1996-97	00.00	00.00	00	89.13	0.38	0.00	89.51
1997-98	63.52	254.08	00	48.19	0.64	0.00	366.43
1998-99	62.56	250.24	00	57.97	1.09	6.00	377.86
1999-2000	100.60	402.49	00	00.00	0.00	0.00	503.09
2000-01	73.26	293.06	00	33.45	11.46	0.00	411.23
	525.00	1808.42	00	534.43	33.45	6.00	2907.3

Source: A&N Forest Department, 2002.

the plywood manufactured in the Andaman Islands is not used locally. It is all exported to mainland India to satisfy the insatiable demands of this ever-increasing market. The government continues to offer various subsidies that include lowly priced local timber, a subsidy to the tune of 90 per cent for the transport of goods to and from the mainland and a power subsidy of over 80 per cent, among others. These subsidies have allowed the timber industry to remain in operation and even make substantial profits. In effect, the exploitation of the forests here is being subsidized for the use and benefit of a faraway population of mainland India that has no real stake in the islands or in the conservation of its forests.

There are other interesting dimensions too. The profits made and the incentives offered by the administration encouraged the plywood mills to go in for substantial augmentation of their production capacities. Today, however, with growing awareness, intervention by the courts and changes in policy, logging in the islands appears to be reducing. Official figures of timber logged shows a downward trend in the last few years (Table 2). Consequently, the amount of timber offered to the plywood mills too has been reduced, leaving the mills complaining about lack of enough timber, resulting in idle capacities. To make up for this shortage in the availability of timber, the private industry has now begun to import timber from Malaysia under the Open General Licencce (OGL) scheme of the Government of India. For the financial year 1997–98, 25 per cent of the private industry intake was met by such imports.

The people who have suffered the most in these islands are the indigenous communities for whom the forests are home. This has resulted from the combined impacts of the destruction of the forests and the imposition of an alien and insensitive culture that brought along with it various diseases and other vices such as alcohol and tobacco consumption.

Except the Nicobarese, all the other tribes have suffered in varying degrees. The Great Andamanese were the first community to be contacted by the British and this was followed by the Onge who live on the island of Little Andaman. Both these communities have suffered immensely from the ill effects of this contact and the interaction that followed.

Table 2. Timber Extraction, Andaman Islands, 1968–2004

Year	Quantity (cu. m)	Year	Quantity (cu. m)
1968–83 (annual average)	118,800	1991–92	105,319
		1992–93	125,670
1980–81	165,726	1993–94	130,136
1981–82	162,241	1994–95	135,523
1982–83	147,308	1995–96	126,579
1983–84	147,309	1996–97	107,443
1984–85	132,579	1997–98	77,097
1985–86	145,305	1998–99	62,623
1986–87	131,888	1999–2000	47,617
1987–88	115,801	2000–01	40,053
1988–89	123,678	2001–02	4,711
1989–90	117,746	2002–03	Nil
1990–91	103,660	2003–04	Nil

Source: Pankaj Sekhsaria and Vishvajit Pandya, *The Jarawa Tribal Reserve Dossier: Cultural and Biological Diversity in the Andaman Islands,* Paris: UNESCO; Pune: Kalpavriksh, 2010, p. 46.

3

FORGOTTEN ISLANDS

The Times of India, 23 May 2007

IF A CERTAIN LINE of beliefs and historical thinking[1] has its way, the Andaman and Nicobar Islands could well see a monumental shift in their present name-scape. The island named after Hugh Rose, the man who finally cornered Rani Lakshmi Bai of Jhansi in 1858, could soon be named Lakshmi Bai Dweep or maybe Rani Jhansi Dweep. Havelock Island named after the British general who retook Lucknow could well be named Nana Sahib Dweep, and the island chain itself should be the Shaheed and Swaraj Islands because that is what Subhas Chandra Bose wanted them to be.

The Rani of Jhansi or Nana Sahib may have known little about the islands but that surely is of no consequence. This group of 500-odd islands, scattered in an arc in the Bay of Bengal, is certainly fertile territory for a massive, even lip-

---

[1] This article was written specifically in response to S. Dasgupta, 'Remembering Kaala Pani', *The Times of India*, 7 May 2007.

smacking renaming exercise – Tantia Tope, Mangal Pandey, Subhas Chandra Bose, Veer Savarkar ... the list is endless, one's imagination being the only limitation – and why not, for reclamation of one's history, after all, is believed to be one of the most important and effective tools of nation building.

There is one hitch, one question, however, that renaming enthusiasts might want to first consider. How do you reclaim what was never yours in the first place? The A&N Islands, located far away from mainland India, can only be considered a gift the British left India when the empire disintegrated.

There are undeniable connections of India's freedom movement with the islands, best symbolized by the revolt of 1857 and the Cellular Jail. Neither can one deny the close bonds that a large section of the country feels with these islands. Yet, all put together, this history does not go beyond 150 years.

We might want to rename Havelock Island in the memory of Nana Sahib, but is it not worth asking whether the island that is today called Havelock had some earlier name too? Can we forget that people have been living here for nearly 40,000 years and places here have all been named by them (Box 1)?

The 150 years that we want to claim now is like the blink of an eye in comparison. Injustices have been done, and continue to be done, to these communities in a manner that has few parallels in India. Their lands have been taken, their forests converted to plywood and agricultural plantations, and the fabric of their societies so violently torn apart that extinction looms on the horizon for many of them.

Box 1: Place names of the Andaman Islands used by the present Great Andamanese tribe

Great Andamanese Place Names[1]		Post-Colonial Names
Khringkosho	A Pujjukar[2] name	Strait Island
Siampsu	A Pujjukar name	An islet by the side of Strait Island
Ilumu Tauro	The island of Onges (Little Andaman)	Little Andaman
Thi-tar-siro	Land near the open sea	Havelock Island
Bilikhu-tara-Phong	Cave of Bilikhu, the supernatural in Great Andamanese	Interview Island
Tebi-Shiro	Shores of the open sea	Neil Island as well as for an island near Mayabundar
Boa	Land	Baratang Island
Lurua	The first fire/flame was found here	Bluff Island
Rait-Phor	Named after the two kinds of bamboos Rait and Phor.	Mayabundar
Mauntenga	Not known	Landfall Island
Sorobul[3]	Dangerous area	Jarawa areas (South Andaman)
Marakele	Present Great Andamanese still use this name	Andaman Archipelago

Great Andamanese Place Names		Post-Colonial Names
Mara Tong	Place where Mar tree is found	A place in Mayabundar where Great Andamanese used to live (now a helipad area)
Lao-tara Nyo	House of evils or foreigners	Port Blair
Jirik-ta Phong	A place where Jirik lives	English Island
Thi-ta-umul	A place with lots of undergrowth	Diglipur

Notes
1. These names are from the present language spoken by the Great Andamanese.
2. Pujjukar is an extinct language once spoken in these islands.
3. Great Andamanese always considered Jarawas dangerous.

Source: Anvita Abbi, *Dictionary of the Great Andamanese Language*, Delhi: Ratna Sagar, 2012, pp. 321–23.

The Great Andamanese, who were at least 5,000 individuals when the 1857 uprising happened, are today down to about fifty people. The Onge who were counted at about 600 in the 1901 census are only about 100 people today. There are critical issues of survival that these communities are faced with, problems that are complex and will be difficult to resolve. If indeed there is energy and interest in doing something positive in the islands and for the islanders, these are the key lines that we need to be thinking on. These are people who, like indigenous peoples everywhere, have their own histories, their own societies, and yes, their own names for the islands and places here.

First, the British called them something else and now, we want to call them something else again. If indeed the places have to be renamed, should not an effort first be made to find out what the original people had named them, why they were so named, what their significance was and which names are still in use by them. Should that not be the work of scholarship and historical studies? It would be a far more challenging and worthwhile exercise, and perhaps not a very difficult one either, because a lot of information already exists in place.

If the real and complete history of the islands is ever written, the British would not be more than a page and India could only be a paragraph. Now, how is that for a perspective and a context?

IN THE SUPREME COURT

4

LOGGING OFF, FOR NOW

Frontline, 18 January 2002

Forestry [in the Andaman Islands] is a comparatively new department for utilizing convict labour and is now the chief source of revenue in cash.

—Lt Col. Richard C. Temple, chief commissioner of the Andaman and Nicobar Islands, in the *Census of India*, 1901

The cutting of naturally grown trees in any [on]going projects [in the Andaman and Nicobar Islands] ... except plantation wood is prohibited.

—Order of the Supreme Court of India, 10 October 2001

THE ANDAMAN AND NICOBAR Islands are clothed in some of the finest tropical evergreen forests in the world and are home to a large number of rare and endangered, even undocumented, species of flora and fauna. It is, however,

23

the classic syndrome of 'missing the wood for the trees' that has driven developmental policies in the islands for over a century. The British first set up the Forest Department here in 1883. For a region so rich in forests, the department's major responsibility, expectedly, was timber extraction. This has gone on unabated ever since, but now a change has been ushered in by the order of the Supreme Court of India dated 10 October 2001.

Forestry operations clearly inflicted large-scale damage to the island's forests, and the biggest losers have been the indigenous communities that have lived and flourished there for thousands of years.

As mentioned earlier, the Great Andamanese, who numbered about 5,000 around the time the operations began, are only about fifty individuals today. The Onge of Little Andaman have suffered a fate that is only marginally better. Timber extraction started here in the 1970s and though their population count has remained steady at around 100 individuals since then, the fabric of their life and society has been tattered. The Jarawas of South and Middle Andaman are better off because until recently they were extremely hostile to the outside world and aggressively defended their forests and way of life. However, this is beginning to change and it is feared that they too will go the way of the Great Andamanese and the Onge. The Sentinelese live on the isolated 100-sq. km North Sentinel Island. They remain hostile and therefore stand the best chance of surviving as an independent human community for some more time.

It was the Onge and the state of their forest home that figured prominently in the Supreme Court's order of 10 October 2001. Investigations in early 1998 had revealed serious violations of their rights, and illegal extraction of timber from the forests of Little Andaman (see Chapter 7). Ironically, the agency responsible in this case was the Andaman and Nicobar Forest Plantation and Development Corporation (ANFPDC), which had been extracting timber since 1977. The main forms of violation included the extraction of timber from within the boundary of the Onge Tribal Reserve, excessive removal of timber from the area where logging was legally permitted and continued logging in the absence of a working plan as required by the Forest Conservation Act (henceforth FCA), 1980, and in violation of an interim order of the Supreme Court dated 12 December 1996 in the Godavarman case.

Based on these findings, three non-governmental organizations – environmental action group Kalpavriksh, the Society for Andaman and Nicobar Ecology (SANE), based in Port Blair, and the Mumbai-based Bombay Natural History Society (BNHS) – filed a writ petition before the Port Blair Circuit Bench of the Calcutta High Court, seeking an end to all logging operations in the island of Little Andaman.

Additional proof of the impact of the forestry operations had been put together by the petitioners. These came from various sources, some relating to Little Andaman in particular and others to the islands in general. For Little Andaman, this included a 1989 study on corals by the Andaman and Nicobar chapter of the Indian National Trust for Art and Cultural Heritage (INTACH). The study showed that the percentage of dead coral was directly related to the level of logging and soil erosion that was taking place on land. In the sea adjoining the main jetty and the timber depot of the island, the relative abundance of live coral was only about 11 per cent.

Other studies showed that endangered fauna like the saltwater crocodile and the endemic Andaman wild pig were being affected owing to logging. The Onge, who critically depend on the wild pig, had reported the same and also asked for the stoppage of logging activities on their island. The most damning critique of forestry operations on the islands as a whole was contained in a 1983 report from the Department of Environment, Government of India. Authors S.C. Nair and Shanthi Nair had argued that the basic assumption underlying the Andaman Canopy-Lifting Shelterwood System (which the Forest Department has been following as a scientific system of forestry) was wrong. This forestry system, they pointed out, was leading to a preponderance of deciduous elements in the evergreen system that would eventually destroy the whole island ecosystem (Box 2).

The Island Development Authority (IDA) too, in its fifth meeting held in 1989 under the chairmanship of the then prime minister, Rajiv Gandhi, resolved that logging had to be phased out over the next few years. As a matter of fact, sensitive officials in the Forest Department have argued all along that forestry operations are not in the best interests of the islands. However, the Forest Department and the local administration continued with large-scale timber extraction.

As far as the petition in the high court was concerned, the Forest Department did what government institutions are best at: they stonewalled it. All that was stated in the writ petition was denied. It was further argued before the judges that the petition had invoked an order from the Supreme Court and the matter could only be argued there. The high court agreed, and the petitioners were forced to approach the Supreme Court through an intervention application filed in 1999 in the *T.N. Godavarman Thirumulpad* vs *the Union of India and others* (Writ Petition 202 [Civil] of 1995).

For over two years, nothing happened as far as the courts (both the Calcutta High Court and the Supreme Court of India) were concerned. On the islands too, things went back to normal after the initial shake-up. The matter finally came up for hearing on 10 October 2001 in the Supreme Court and, in a significant order, a bench comprising Justices B.N. Kirpal, Santosh Hegde and Ashok Bhan stayed the 'felling of naturally grown trees in the entire area' of the Andaman and Nicobar Islands.

That the timber extraction operations involve crores of rupees annually is common knowledge. There have also been allegations that many top forest officers and administrators have made a lot of money through illegal extraction and transport of timber. Concrete proof of this was unearthed in February 2000, even as the issue of illegal logging was pending before the Supreme Court. The matter involved the issue of unnumbered transit passes for the transport of nearly 400 cubic metres of timber from Mayabundar in North Andaman to Chennai, and even though Bishnu Pada Ray, member of parliament from the islands, wrote to the chief vigilance commissioner demanding a probe, nothing has come of it yet. At a conservative estimate, the total consignment was worth over ₹2.7 million and it is being described as only the tip of the iceberg.

Significantly, the demand for timber from industries on the islands has been falling steadily over the last few years. A look at the figures show that while timber to the extent of 47,617 cu. m was legally logged in 1999–2000, the figure fell to 40,053 cu. m in 2000–01 (Table 2). Importantly, an increasingly large quantity of the timber was not being lifted by the industries that it was meant for. In 1999–2000, 25 per cent of the timber logged was not lifted, while in 2000–01 nearly 42 per cent remained in the depots of the Forest Department. The fact that this reality was not taken into account while setting extraction targets for the following year is a clear indication that there are other forces at play.

Following the 10 October 2001 order, the matter came up for hearing again before a bench comprising justices B.N. Kirpal, K.G. Balakrishnan and Arijit Pasayat on 23 November. In addition to the stay on felling of naturally grown trees, the bench directed that, 'no sawmill, plywood or veneer factory shall utilize any naturally grown trees without further orders from this court'. The court also appointed an expert commission under Professor Shekhar Singh of the New Delhi–based Indian Institute of Public Administration (IIPA) to look into the state of the forests and other related matters on the islands.

There has been some degree of resentment over the complete stoppage of forestry-related activities on the islands, particularly because of the implications on the livelihoods of those involved. Figures for 1997–98 show that there were thirty-five timber-based industries on the islands. These included three private plywood mills, two government sawmills, nineteen private sawmills and eleven match/pencil and composite units. The three plywood mills employed about 3,000 individuals and used a large chunk (nearly 65 per cent) of the timber that was cut on the islands. Over the last year or so, two of these big mills, employing an estimated 2,000 persons, shut down, citing financial and administrative reasons. Other smaller units too have not been functional.

The net result was that in 2000–01 only 24,000 cu. m of timber was picked up for use when the total quantity that had been cut was over 40,000 cu. m.

The 1991 census figures had put the total number of workers in the islands at about 91,000 individuals. Those involved in forestry (including activities such as planting, replanting and conservation work) were estimated at around 10 per cent of the islands' total workforce. Latest figures for the operational industries in the islands, their capacities and people employed are reportedly being put together by the administration as demanded by the court.

At the same time, there is another large body of opinion that sees in these developments a new chapter for the islands and the islanders. That forestry could not have gone on forever is well known and the challenge now lies in finding creative and more sustainable solutions. There are a number of areas of work that are directly related to the forests that have the potential to provide employment to a large number of people. This includes water and soil conservation activities, social forestry and regenerating degraded forest lands, agro-forestry and a better level of wildlife conservation and protection work. Fisheries have great potential, thanks to the fish-rich seas that surround the islands. An effort needs to be made towards sustained and sustainable utilization of these resources.

The court order comes at a significant juncture in the context of the ongoing preparation of the National Biodiversity Strategy and Action Plan. Coordinated on the islands by the Andaman and Nicobar Islands Environmental Team (ANET), the draft plan was released recently. It points out that the biggest issue confronting the islands today is the rapid population growth as a result of large-scale migration from mainland India. The present estimated population of the islands is 500,000.[1] If one were to consider just the availability of drinking water there, it will become clear that the carrying capacity of the islands has long been exceeded.

Agricultural yields in the islands have fallen and evidence from other tropical forest regions of the world shows that these soils are not conducive to agricultural activities. A horticulture-based system might have some answers. Tourism on the islands is growing rapidly and is being seen as the next big revenue earner. However, the draft plan identifies tourism as a cause for concern, unless steps are taken to ensure that it is environment-friendly. There are other issues on the islands as well. There is large-scale encroachment of the forests, the mangrove cover has fallen substantially over the last few decades and coral reefs have been impacted by land-based activities such as logging, agriculture and pesticide use. All this is critically linked to the precious biodiversity of these islands, on which the lives and livelihood of their people depend.

The Biodiversity Strategy and Action Plan (BSAP) has the potential to create a broad framework in which the future of the islands can be discussed, debated and planned. In many ways, the mandate of the BSAP for the islands and the mandate before the commission appointed by the court overlap neatly. There are many burning issues that have to be dealt with if the future of the islands is to be secured. Logging, though critical, is only one of them. The challenge now is to find a creative way forward.

---

[1] The number was an estimate based on an informal assessment of the situation on the ground. The official population figure according to the 2001 census was 3,56,265 (Table 3).

Box 2: The Andaman Canopy-Lifting Shelterwood System

The concentrated 'natural generation' with the help of Andaman Canopy Lifting Shelterwood System to obtain a more uniform crop now widely practised in Andaman forests is a practice that is tending to convert evergreen forests into deciduous forests, while all plywood and matchwood demand is for softwood from evergreen forests. A closer look at the canopy-lifting method would clarify this point ...

The foresters apparently believe that the natural vegetation of these islands needs human assistance to perpetuate, as its regeneration, indicated by younger-class density, is very low. This is totally wrong. The low younger-class density only reflects the stability of the plant community, the slow growth rate and complex structuring of the forest. Most of the seedlings and understorey plants that survive naturally are evergreen, indicating that through plant succession or plant community evolution, the deciduous nature of vegetation is changing to evergreen ... Hence, the basic assumption underlying canopy-lifting management is wrong and the operation can only destroy the whole island system ... By the canopy-lifting system, the entire floral composition is altered and more gregarious strands of select species are encouraged to grow. This method is not congenial for species conservation in an evergreen biotope ...

A species normally is an integrated component in a community and only with the total milieu of that community can it successfully survive. This milieu is produced together by all the components of that community. If it is modified so drastically that its intrinsic physico-chemical and biological conditions are changed, many of the individual evergreen species may not survive in the modified environment ... The whole principle underlying the Canopy-Lifting Shelterwood System assumes a fairly closed canopy even after felling, and a fairly dense understorey too. But actually, after the extraction work, there is very little canopy remaining, and the balance sparse cover is even further thinned. This exposes the previously closed forest floor to sunlight and weeds gain entry. Increased entry of sunlight dries up the soil and heavy rain erodes and carries away all the humus-rich top soil. Seedlings of evergreen species fail to germinate and establish themselves. Poor reserves of soil nutrients and less humid conditions inevitably initiate rapid retrogression of the area ...

In other words, the entire evergreen forest cover of these islands is changing to deciduous because of this management practice. Besides, there is the moot point whether under the bioclimatic and physical environmental condition obtained in the Andaman Islands, a deciduous forest ecosystem can remain viable without undergoing further retrogression. This is apart from the irreparable harm it is causing to forests with over 2,300 species of flowering plants already listed, among which endemism is very high, and where nearly a hundred species reported earlier cannot be located in their type localities now.

For about twenty species of timber value, a forest of infinitesimally greater value and diversity has been lost sight of.

This note is an edited extract from Satish Nair and Shanthi Nair, *Report of the Project for Formulating a Land Evaluation Survey of Andaman and Nicobar Islands*, New Delhi: Department of Environment, Government of India, 1983.

5

TO SAVE AN ARCHIPELAGO

Frontline, 21 June 2002

ON 7 MAY 2002, the Supreme Court of India, while hearing a matter relating to the environment of the Andaman and Nicobar Islands, accepted the recommendations of the Shekhar Singh Commission it had appointed to look into the issues involved and passed a set of landmark orders.

The commission had made a number of major recommendations (Appendx I) ranging from a ban on all tree felling in the islands, except for the bona fide use of the local islander populations; a ban on transport of timber to any part of the country; removal of encroachments; steps to reduce immigration from mainland India; shutting down of the Andaman and Nicobar Forest Plantation and Development Corporation (ANFPDC) that had logged the forests of Little Andaman Island for years; phasing out of the existing monoculture plantations of red oil palm, rubber and teak; closing down of the Andaman Trunk Road (ATR) in the Jarawa Tribal Reserve areas; and a stop to sand mining from the island's beaches. The court's orders offer the best chance to save the rich but threatened tropical rainforests and the vulnerable indigenous communities of these unique islands. The orders will also have far-reaching implications for the immigrant populations that have settled here from the mainland.

The larger proceedings are part of the *T.N. Godavarman Thirumulpad* vs *The Union of India and Ors* (Writ Petition 202 [Civil] of 1995), better known as the 'Forest Case'. The orders came in a specific intervention filed jointly before the apex court in 1999 by SANE, BNHS and the environmental action group Kalpavriksh, with the support of the Environmental Justice Initiative (EJI) and the Human Rights Law Network (HRLN).

During a hearing on 23 November 2001, the court had appointed the one-man Shekhar Singh Commission '... to look into the state of the island's forests and other related matters', and submit its recommendations within six weeks. Shekhar Singh, who has considerable experience in working on issues concerning the islands, submitted a voluminous three-part report to the court on 18 February 2002.

Understandably, there was strong opposition to some parts of the report. A flurry of activity followed, which saw a number of other parties including the Andaman Furniture Industries Association (AFIA), the Andaman and Nicobar Islands Small-Scale Wood-based Industries Association (ANISSWIA) and the member of parliament from the islands, Bishnu Pada Ray, in addition to the local administration and the Union Ministry of Environment and Forests (MoEF) filing affidavits. The general opinion in the islands favoured the shutting down of timber extraction and export operations. However, recommendations to close down the ATR and phase out the sand-mining operations, both of which would affect a major chunk of the business operators here, were strongly opposed. The islands have a prominent sand mafia that has great political and financial muscle. Today, the sand-mining industry that feeds the rapidly growing construction boom of Port Blair is posing one of the biggest environmental problems in the islands and drastic solutions are required to address the issue.

A lot of the coordinated opposition materialized in a call for a complete bandh in Port Blair by the Andaman Chamber of Commerce and Industries (ACCI) on 12 March 2002. All political parties including the Congress (I), the Bharatiya Janata Party (BJP) and the Dravida Munnetra Kazhagam (DMK), and a number of trader and business organizations supported the bandh call. That the bandh and the opposition to the recommendations did not have universal support became evident in the next few days. In their statements dated 16 March and 18 March respectively, the Local-Borns Association (LBA) (descendants of penal settlers) and the Bengal Association of Andaman and Nicobar Islands (BAANI) strongly supported the commission's recommendations. The BAANI statement said: 'There has been some discontent and opposition to the recommendations of the commission and a fear ... that this will adversely impact the people and the socio-economic situation in the islands. We, on the other hand, feel that the recommendations are ... in the best interests of the people and the environment here. The fears expressed are either out of a vested interest or an incorrect reading and interpretation of the recommendations.'

It was on 7 May 2002, just a couple of days before the Supreme Court went into vacation that the matter came up before a bench comprising Chief Justice B.N. Kirpal and Justices Arijit Pasayat and H.K. Sema. The solicitor general and amicus curiae in the case, Harish Salve, argued forcefully for the uniqueness and importance of the forests and the islands that have been designated as a 'global biodiversity hot spot' and the urgent need for their conservation.

Thereafter, the bench issued orders (see Appendix II) accepting the report of the Shekhar Singh Commission, while making some 'not very major' modifications (except in the matter of sand mining). While the commission had suggested that sand mining be disallowed from September 2002, the final order of the court says that it should be phased out at a minimum rate of 20 per cent every year, so as to bring it down to 33 per cent of the present level in five years.

Families that have been identified as having encroached on forest land prior to 1978, and that had either not moved to their allotted sites or had occupied more land than they were entitled to, were given one month to make the necessary corrections. The commission had recommended that all post-1978 encroachments be removed within six months and that the displaced families be allotted homesteads on revenue land. The court order reduced this time limit to three months.

Further, the court ordered that the licences of all private sawmills and wood-based industries in the islands be terminated with effect from 31 March 2003. It ordered that the 'Working Plans' for limited timber extraction for local use be reformulated and submitted to the court within twelve weeks. In an important step that should set a precedent for the rest of the country, the court also directed that the working plans be formulated by a committee that has one ecologist proficient with the islands' ecology.

Environmental and tribal rights groups from across the country and abroad too have welcomed the Supreme Court's orders. The timing of the orders is also significant. That summer, large parts of Port Blair were being supplied piped drinking water for a mere twenty minutes, once every three days. Evidently, the Supreme Court of India cannot rectify this situation, but part of the long-term solution to this critical problem may well be achieved through the sincere implementation of its orders. That, however, is easier said than done and we have to wait to see what eventually happens.

6

ANDAMAN'S LAST CHANCE

The Hindu Survey of the Environment 2003

THE SUPREME COURT OF India (SC) proposes, the local administration disposes. This cliché perhaps best describes the present situation in the Andaman and Nicobar Islands. Going beyond clichés, the matter is an extremely serious one. In response to an intervention related to the islands filed in the Godavarman case, the apex court of the country had passed detailed orders in May 2002 (Appendices I and II). Most are of extreme significance to the fragile environment and the threatened indigenous communities of these islands, but the administration carries on as if nothing has happened. The deadlines are long gone; yet, unfortunately, some of the key orders continue to remain unimplemented.

The orders of the court were comprehensive and wide-ranging. The court even prescribed a clear time frame for implementing many of the orders. The ATR, for example, was to be shut down in three months. This was also the time limit for the declaration of the Inner Line Area, while the islanders' identity cards were to be issued within six months. For the petitioners, environmental groups and those fighting for the rights of the indigenous peoples in the islands, it seemed like a big step forward. It has, however, taken only a few months for all to realize that it is one thing to get the court to pass orders and completely another to get them implemented.

The two specific issues that clearly highlight this are those related to the closing of the ATR and declaring the islands as an Inner Line Area. Over the years, the islands have seen large-scale migration of people from the mainland. Not only has this severely marginalized the indigenous people here, but the influx is also severely stretching the capacity of the islands to even sustain the settlers who have now made the islands their home. It is solely in the interest of the people who are already here that further migration be stopped.

A lot of discussion and thought have gone into this particular problem for many years, and the overall consensus has been that declaring the islands as an Inner Line Area along with the issuance of islanders' identity cards stands the best chance of resolving the situation. The court ordered the administration to declare the Inner Line in three months and allowed an additional three months to complete the process for the issuing of identity cards. The local administration did start the process for the identity cards, but no attempt was (or is being) made to sort out the issues related to the Inner Line declaration. As a result, the identity cards process too could not be completed and it is now more than seven months since the deadline for the Inner Line declaration has passed.

The influx of people, meanwhile, continues unabated. The lietenant governor and chief administrator of this Union

territory, N.N. Jha, seems less than willing to follow this order
of the court as is evident from his statement published in the
12 January 2003 issue of the *Week*: 'If we were to keep on
creating such inner lines, every district in India would end
up with a restricted area. It would affect fisheries and other
local commercial activities.'

The other example is that of the ATR, the shutting down
of which is critical to ensure the survival of the Jarawa
community and the forests of the Jarawa Reserve. The
ATR cuts through the heart of the forests that the Jarawas
call home and has become the most crucial vector bringing
many unwanted influences to the Jarawas. These include an
epidemic of measles in 1999, consumption of tobacco and
alcohol that the Jarawa are slowly getting addicted to, a huge
tourist influx and sexual exploitation as well. Significantly,
the Jarawa Reserve has the last remaining patch of tropical
evergreen forests on the main Andaman Islands. It is indeed
in the best interest of the Jarawas that these forests stay
strictly protected, and many believe that only the Jarawas
can best protect these forests.

It was keeping this in mind that the order for shutting
down the road in three months had been passed by the court.
If the response of the administration were anything to go by,
it would seem the SC never passed any orders of this kind.
Presently, the road is being repaired, and a huge passenger
hall is under construction (as of February 2003) on that part
of the road which the SC has ordered shut. The member of
parliament from the islands, meanwhile, is addressing public
meetings demanding that the ATR be declared a national
highway and assuring people that work for making it a
double-lane highway will be started shortly.

The petitioners have repeatedly brought this situation to the notice of the authorities concerned, through the Central Empowered Committee (CEC) set up by the apex court to deal with matters in the Godavarman case. In three affidavits filed before the CEC, in September 2002 and in January and March 2003, respectively, details of the violations and the expiry of the time frame for implementation have been clearly indicated.

Other concerned citizens and NGOs too have taken up the matter. In a letter sent to the CEC, the prime minister and the president of the country in January 2003, the All India Coordinating Forum for Adivasis and Indigenous people (AICFAIP) has pointed out that by not implementing the orders of the SC, '... the [A&N] administration is wilfully letting off a historical opportunity, one for which they alone will not be held responsible but the Central Government [will be held responsible] as well. The non-implementation of the orders of the SC by the A&N administration is not only extremely detrimental for the Jarawas, the Onges and the forests of the islands, it is also in complete disregard of the legal system of the country and a clear violation of the orders of the Supreme Court.' The communication further states: 'It is indeed shocking that the A&N administration is continuing in clear and wilful disregard of the highest court in the country, an act that can amount to contempt, that should be the responsibility of the highest officers in the administration here.' The A&N administration, however, seems adamant about not implementing these orders. They have themselves filed before the SC a petition asking for a review of the orders, but importantly, this has been done many months after the timelines have passed.

What is perhaps most significant is the fact that these orders offer an excellent opportunity for environmental protection and conservation in these fragile islands, and could well become the model for others in the country to look up to. It is an opportunity that should have been grabbed with both hands, but what we continue to see is its wilful squandering.[1]

---

[1] The order for the closure of the Andaman Trunk Road has not been implemented even as of 2016. For more details and a further discussion on the issue see Chapters 11, 12 and 13.

INDIGENOUS
PEOPLES

THE ONGE

7

A PEOPLE IN PERIL

Frontline, 7 May 1999

ON 26 FEBRUARY 1999, *Andaman Herald*, a Port Blair newspaper, reported that the bodies of two young members of the Onge tribal community were found floating in a creek near their Dugong Creek settlement on Little Andaman Island. The young men had been missing for a few days, apparently, after having gone turtle-hunting. The cause of the deaths was not known, but drowning was ruled out. The Onge people are excellent swimmers and sailors, and there is no record of an Onge drowning in a creek. The newspaper said that foul play was suspected as the post-mortem and cremation were done with undue haste. Additionally, one of the dead men had reportedly complained to an adviser to the Planning Commission, who visited the island in the recent past, about the resource depletion that the community faced owing to illegal timber logging and poaching in the forests.

The incident assumes significance in the light of the fact that the Onge issue has a complex history. A powerful two-pronged attack – on the natural resource base that sustains the community and on the culture of the community – has, over the past three decades, slowly but surely pushed the Onges to a point of no return. Recent investigations in Little Andaman have brought to light some glaring irregularities, and the two reported deaths are believed to be the latest and the most obvious consequence of the process.

The story of the Onge people's alienation began in the late 1960s, when the Government of India planned a massive development and colonization programme for the Union territory of the Andaman and Nicobar Islands in complete disregard of the fragile environment of the islands and the rights of the tribal communities. A 1965 plan, prepared specifically for Little Andaman, proposed the clear-felling of nearly 40 per cent of the island's forests, the bringing in of 12,000 settler families to the island and the promotion of commercial plantations such as those of red oil palm, and timber-based industries in order to support the settler population (Box 3).

Logistical problems, lack of infrastructure and a revision of policies over time ensured that the plan was not fully implemented. Even in its partial implementation and the very conception and planning of the development programme, the Onges had been sidelined and the violations initiated.

Box 3: The main targets to be achieved in the
development of Little Andaman Island

i)   Clearance of 60,000 acres of forest land
ii) Settlement of 12,000 families on agriculture (including
     plantation, horticulture, etc.)
iii) Establishment of an integrated industrial complex based
     on timber resources of the island
iv) Establishment of a sugar factory with an annual capacity
     of 60,000–70,000 tonnes

Source: *Report by the interdepartmental team on the Accelerated
Development Programme for Andaman and Nicobar Islands*,
New Delhi: Ministry of Rehabilitation, Government of India,
1965, p. 123.

The government team that suggested the development
programme completely ignored the Andaman and Nicobar
Protection of Aboriginal Tribes Regulation (ANPATR),
which had in 1957 accorded the status of a tribal reserve to
the entire island of Little Andaman. Further, about 20,000
hectares (roughly 30 per cent) of the island was de-notified
from its tribal reserve status in two stages, in 1972 and
1977, still leaving 52,000 ha as an inviolable tribal reserve
(see Map 2). Many of the proposed projects were also taken
up for implementation. These included a 1,600-ha red oil
palm plantation and a major timber extraction operation
that continues even today.[1]

---

[1] The timber extraction in Little Andaman was stopped following
Supreme Court orders in 2001 (see Chapters 4 and 5).

The Forest Department leased out 19,600 ha from the de-notified area to the Andaman and Nicobar Forest Plantation and Development Corporation, which is the sole agency responsible for timber extraction here. In 1976, the ANFPDC presented its 'Project Report for Logging and Marketing of Timber' from the forests of Little Andaman. It was estimated that a total of 60,000 ha of the island was available for logging and that 60,000 cu. m of timber could be extracted annually from 800 ha.

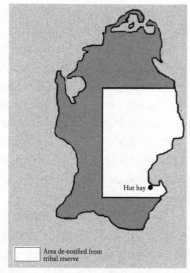

Map 2: Little Andaman Island

Here again was another clear violation of the Onge tribal reserve. When an area of 52,000 ha of the island's total area of 73,000 ha was already a tribal reserve, how could 60,000 ha be made available for logging? ANFPDC should have limited its operations to the 19,600 ha that had been leased out to it. With 1,600 ha being under red oil palm plantation, the actual area for logging was even less. This meant that ANFPDC should have logged only 18,000 cu. m of timber from an area of 240 ha annually. The average for the actual logging over the last two decades, however, is much higher – at 25,000 cu. m of timber from an area of 400 ha annually.

Furthermore, a working plan has not been prepared for the logging operations on Little Andaman, and the continued logging contravenes a Supreme Court ruling of 1996, which had ordered the stopping of all logging in the absence of such a plan. The Forest Department has justified the logging on the basis of its 1976 project report. However, the legality and validity of this report are open to question. Significantly, the deputy conservator of forests (Working Plan) (DCF-WP) of the Andaman and Nicobar Forest Department is now preparing a working plan for the forests of Little Andaman. This clearly contradicts the present stand of the department, which claims that the equivalent of a working plan already exists.

As if this was not enough, ANFPDC has gone a step further; it is logging within the tribal reserve, making a mockery of the law and also the rights of the Onges. Maps available with ANFPDC and the Forest Department have logging coupes dated 1990 onwards marked clearly within the tribal reserve.

Even as these violations have continued, thousands of outsiders have been settled in Little Andaman. The settler population grew rapidly – from a few hundred in the 1960s to 7,000 in 1984 and over 12,000 in 1991 – displacing Onges from some of their most preferred habitats. Hut Bay, the main town in the island, is a prime example.

The Andaman Adim Janjati Vikas Samiti (AAJVS), the official tribal welfare body of the administration, introduced welfare measures that were completely unsuitable for the Onges. Foodstuff such as rice, dal, oil and biscuits were introduced to a community whose traditional food included the meat of the wild boar and turtle, fish, tubers and honey. The agency even offered each adult 250 gm of tobacco as a 'welfare' measure. In a blatant attempt to move the forestry operations deeper into the forests of Little Andaman, the authorities have sought to settle the nomadic Onges at Dugong Creek in the north-east of the island and at South Bay at the southern tip. Wooden houses on stilts and with asbestos roofing were constructed for them at these places. These structures were not suited for the hot and humid tropical environment of the islands, and the Onge people preferred to live in their traditional huts in the forest nearby.

Simultaneously, attempts were made to introduce a cash economy in a community that did not have even a barter system. Ill-conceived schemes, such as the raising of a coconut plantation (in which the Onge people were made workers), cattle rearing (the community does not consume milk) and pig breeding were introduced. All of them failed. Environmentalist Bittu Sahgal noted that during one of his visits to the Onge settlement a few years ago, the Onge people were being asked to do menial chores such as fetching water for welfare workers appointed by the administration. A visit to the Onge settlement of Dugong Creek has become mandatory on many a VIP itinerary. Not only are the Onge people expected to perform for the pleasure and entertainment of the VIP, but they are also put to work weeks in advance to tidy up the settlement.

The settler communities, which have been handed over the lands and resources of the Onge people, have not treated them any better. They exploit and look down upon the tribal people. Alcohol was introduced and many Onges have become addicts. This addiction is now exploited – the Onge exchange with the settlers valuable resources, such as honey, turtle eggs, wild boar meat and ambergris, for liquor.

Logging operations have also helped open up the forests, encouraging further encroachments into the tribal reserve. Consequently, illegal activities such as poaching have become rampant, resulting in a drastic decline of creatures such as the monitor lizard, the dugong and the endemic Andaman wild pig. All these creatures are not only important sources of food and nutrition for the Onge people, but they also play an integral role in their culture and society. Their unavailability leaves gaps that simply cannot be filled.

It is clear now that the survival of the Onges can only be ensured if the present policies vis-à-vis development and the tribal people are reviewed with sensitivity. Serious attention must be paid to what the tribal people have to say and an honest attempt made to find out what they want. There are no signs of that being done though. (See Boxes 4 and 5 respectively for a chronology of developments in Little Andaman and for an idea of the wealth of knowledge and experience of the Onge.)

At a meeting of the District Planning Committee held in Port Blair in November 1998, the Onge representative, Tambolai, complained that settlers living in the areas near their settlement were troubling them. A major point he made was that finding wild pigs in the forests was becoming difficult and hence the timber extraction operations should be stopped.

If the responses of the authorities are indeed anything to go by, Tambolai may well have been talking to the wind.

Box 4: Little Andaman: A chronology

1867	Attack by the Onge on the British ship *Assam Valley*.
1880	Little Andaman is visited by British officer M.V. Portman.
1901	*Population of the Onge 672.*
1921	*Population of the Onge 346.*
1951	*Population of the Onge 150.*
	Little Andaman is visited by Italian anthropologist Cipriani to study the Onge.
1957	Declaration of Onge Tribal Reserve including the islands of Little Andaman, Rutland, Cinque, North Brother, South Brother and Sisters.
1961	*Population of the Onge 129.*
1965	Report by the the interdepartmental team on Accelerated Development Programme for the A&N Islands, Ministry of Rehabilitation, Government of India.
1969	366 East Pakistan families settled in Little Andaman.
1970	Survey for the establishment of red oil palm plantation.
1970	First sawmill is set up on the island; annual intake 2,000 cu. m of timber.
1971	*Population of the Onge 112.*
1972	First amendment to the tribal reserve.
1973	165 Nicobari families settled in Harmander Bay area on the island.
	Forest Department (FD) assessment of timber productivity of the island's forests.
1975	FD initiates work on the oil palm plantation.
1975–76	Creation of the first 160 ha of oil palm plantation.
1976	Creation of the Andaman Adim Janjati Vikas Samiti (Andaman Tribal Welfare Society).

	Presentation of Andaman and Nicobar Forest Plantation and Development Corporation (ANFPDC) proposal for logging and forestry operations in Little Andaman.
1977	ANFPDC starts functioning.
1977	Second amendment to the tribal reserve.
1977–79	118 families from mainland settled on Little Andaman.
1981	*Population of the Onge: 100.*
1983	Study of the Onge by anthropologist Vishvajit Pandya.
1990	Master plan for the development of the tribes of the islands by S.A. Awaradi.
1991	Final amendment to the tribal reserve.
1991	*Population of the Onge 101.*
1996	Patenting controversy related to Onge knowledge.
1996	Supreme Court of India ruling on forests.

Box 5: A precious heritage

The ethnobotanical knowledge of the Onge tribal community is impressive. Italian anthropologist Lidio Cipriani, who studied the community in the 1950s, was among the first of many experts to acknowledge this Onge heritage. He wrote in 1966: 'In their continual search for food, the Onges have acquired botanical and zoological knowledge which seems almost innate, and they know of properties in plants and animals of which we are quite unaware. Nearly every day on Little Andaman I came across this. I had only to draw a rough sketch of an animal and they knew at once where it could be found; it was only thanks to them that I was able to find the various amphibia, which subsequently proved to be new species.'

Among the best-known examples of Onge knowledge is the method they use to extract honey from the hives of the giant rock bee. In order to ward off the bees, they use the leaves of a plant, which they call *tonjoghe* (*Orphea katshalica*). To quote Cipriani again: '... the juice of a certain plant they call *tonjoghe* ... has the power of deterring bees, and this knowledge (which) has been handed down from generation to generation, is applied with delightful simplicity ... There are bushes of *tonjoghe* everywhere ... the Onges simply grab a handful of leaves and stuff them into the mouth. With some vigorous chewing they are quickly reduced to a greenish pulp, which is smeared all over the body ... Another huge mouthful is chewed on the way up and spat at the bees to make sure that they will be deterred ... The bees fly away from the comb without stinging and the honey can be cut out ...' causing harm neither to the collector of honey nor to the bees.

Disregarding such knowledge, attempts are made to impart modern technology to the Onge people. A few years ago, the Fisheries Department posted a fisheries inspector and two fishermen at Dugong Creek to teach Onges modern methods of fishing. The fishermen admitted later they had much to learn from the tribals about fishing in the waters of the island.

More recently, a controversy erupted when senior researchers from the Indian Council of Medical Research (ICMR) tried to patent a discovery that would probably lead to a cure for cerebral malaria. The issue attracted international attention. The source of the medicine in question is a plant that the Onge use to treat fever and stomach disorders.

The size and nature of the wealth that lies in the island home of the Onge people are largely unknown. What is more important is that if the present situation continues, the Onge people may themselves not survive for too long and with them will go a huge bank of invaluable knowledge.

—*Frontline*, 7 May 1999

THE JARAWA

8

JARAWA EXCURSIONS

Frontline, 17 July 1998

IN OCTOBER 1997, SETTLERS in the Middle Andaman Island were witness to an unfamiliar sight: a group of unarmed Jarawas had ventured out of the forest and into modern settlements on the fringes of the forests. This was among the first recorded instances of Jarawas voluntarily seeking to establish contact with the settlers from mainland India. It was particularly puzzling given the fact that Jarawas have for long been hostile towards the settlers. To them they have lost large swathes of their forests, and the tribal people have fiercely defended what is left of their traditional lands.

Over the next few months, there were several more reports of Jarawas coming out of their forests. Some of them, it was reported, were seen to point to their bellies: this was interpreted as an expression of hunger and in the belief that they had run out of their traditional food resources in the forests and were facing starvation, the local administration, led by Lieutenant Governor I.P. Gupta, arranged for food relief.

Packets containing dry fish, puffed rice and bananas were air-dropped from helicopters into Jarawa territory. The natural resources that the Jarawas have had access to have vastly diminished over time for a number of reasons, including widespread deforestation to accommodate settlers and to feed the flourishing timber industry. Even so, the theory that starvation is driving the Jarawas out of the forests appears to be flawed. They have sustained themselves on forest produce for centuries, and there is no reason to believe that they have suddenly been pushed into starvation. In any case, eyewitnesses say that the Jarawas who were sighted recently appear to be healthy, robust and agile. Moreover, in February and March 1998, no person from the tribal community approached the settlements for extended periods, that is, for more than two weeks. And when they did show up, it was often in small groups of five to ten people.

Anthropologists, however, have another explanation for the Jarawas' curious 'coming out'. It relates to the experience of Enmey, a teenaged Jarawa boy who was found with a fractured foot near Kadamtala town in Middle Andaman last year. The local residents, most of them settlers, arranged for his treatment at the G.B. Pant Hospital in Port Blair, where he was looked after well. When Enmey recovered, he was sent back to Middle Andaman, where he promptly disappeared into his forest home. Since October, it is Enmey who has largely been responsible for bringing his people out.

Anthropologists explain that Enmey developed a cultural affinity to the outside world: in their view, Enmey perhaps wanted others in his community to experience the settlers' hospitality that he had had a taste of. It is this, and not starvation, that had drawn them out of the forests, they reason. This is, perhaps, in addition to the pressures that the Jarawas are experiencing from multiple sources. Today, there are only about 250[1] of them and vast expanses of their rainforest homelands have been cleared to accommodate settlers and to feed the huge timber industry on which rests the economic foundation of the Andamans.

In order to protect the Jarawa way of life, a Jarawa tribal reserve was established initially in 1957 and then extended to over a 1,000-sq. km area in 2004; the objective was as much to keep the tribal population confined to the reserve as to prevent settlers from encroaching upon it. Along the periphery of the reserve, forty-four bush police camps were established with about 400 policemen. Over time, however, several encroachments were made and the function of the police force has become one of confining the Jarawas, who once roamed the length and breadth of the island unhindered, to the reserve area. Over the years the area of the Jarawa Tribal Reserve has gone on shrinking. This is depicted in Map 3.

The 340-km-long Andaman Trunk Road, which slices through the heart of the Jarawa Reserve, has opened up more areas for settlement. Right from the beginning, the Jarawas had protested against the construction of the road on the grounds that it would endanger their way of life. They set up road blocks, demolished bridges and even attacked – and occasionally killed – the workers. Work came to a halt in

---

[1] This was an estimated figure; the actual Jarawa population based on a complete count and as reported in the 2011 census is 380 (Table 4).

1976, but was resumed soon. Traffic on the road, which was completed recently, has grown enormously.

Today, many more settlers live in the areas bordering the reserve, thereby increasing manifold the possibility of

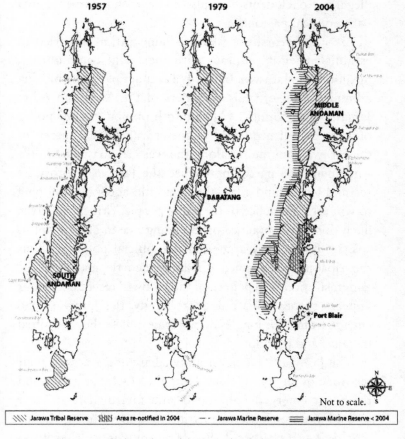

Map 3: Changes in the boundary of the Jarawa Tribal Reserve over the years.
Source: *The Jarawa Tribal Reserve Dossier: Cultural and Biological Diversity in the Andaman Islands*, UNESCO & Kalpavriksh, 2010

interaction and conflict between them and the Jarawas. Instances of people trespassing into the reserve to hunt wild boar and deer, and to poach forest produce such as honey and timber, are common. At times, the trespassers destroy the rudimentary settlements of the Jarawas. In addition, many illegal encroachments have also come up in the reserve area with political patronage.

Over the years, the island administration has tried to establish friendly contact with the tribal communities, including the Jarawas. In 1974, a contact party comprising administration officials, members of the Andaman Adim Janjati Vikas Samiti (AAJVS), anthropologists and police officials, established friendly contact with some members of the Jarawa community along the western coast of Middle Andaman. The party approached the Jarawa territory by sea and left behind gifts – bananas and coconuts – hoping to win the confidence of the tribal people. Critics, however, liken this to the practice of scattering rice in an attempt to ensnare birds. They argue that the official policy vis-à-vis the tribal people is aimed at making them dependent on the administration. The pattern of the Jarawas' recent behaviour appears to bear this out; increasingly, the Jarawas who emerge from their jungles do not leave unless they are gifted bananas and coconuts.

The Jarawas have never allowed anyone access to their territory by the land route. Nor, until October 1997, had they ever emerged voluntarily and unarmed from their forest homes or initiated any interaction with the outside world. The October 1997 development is, therefore, very significant, but the administration has not always responded with sensitivity to the Jarawas' needs. An incident which this writer witnessed on 9 April 1998 illustrates this point.

At 8 a.m. that day, about sixty Jarawas, the largest group yet to emerge from the jungle, arrived at the Uttara jetty near Kadamtala. Among them were several children and women with babies. It is, of course, true that the administration has no way of knowing where and when the next group of Jarawas will turn up or just how many of them will be there, but even so, there appeared to be little evidence of planning for such contingencies. Until such time as coconuts and bananas could be arranged for the Jarawas, they were herded into a small waiting hall at the jetty and made to wait on that hot, sweltering day without food or water. The only people at the jetty who seemed equipped to handle the situation were a policeman and three boatmen who knew some of the Jarawa people. But after a while, when the Jarawas grew restive, even the boatmen ran out of ideas. Things got a bit rough, and there was a fair bit of shoving and pushing around, which the Jarawas resented fiercely.

The consignment of coconuts and bananas that the local police had organized arrived around 2 p.m. Each person in the Jarawa group was given two coconuts and a bunch of bananas. The entire group was then put on boats and, escorted by armed policemen, taken back into Jarawa territory. At the other end, however, more trouble was in store. Just as one of the boatmen was about to return, some of the Jarawa youth, who were evidently incensed by the way they had been treated that afternoon, seized the boatman's bamboo pole as he was pushing back his boat and tried to haul him ashore. The shaken boatman said later that evening: 'I have interacted with the Jarawa people for twelve years, but for the first time in my life I was afraid. I did not know what they would do to me.' However, some of the older women of the tribe, who had known the boatman for long, admonished the youth and forced them to let him go. Had any bodily harm been done to the boatman, the consequences would have been unpredictable. The settlers, already restive over the constant 'intrusion' by Jarawas, might well have retaliated violently.

Administration officials admit in private that they are unable to do anything to ease the tension between the tribal communities and the settlers. The two groups are locked in a tussle over land rights, and the atmosphere has been vitiated by administrative policies of the past. The Jarawas, as the original inhabitants, have the first right over this land, but not many people are willing to concede this. The tension can be eased if the settlements of the outsiders are removed from in and around the Jarawa territory. But this requires tremendous political will and understanding, which is absent.

If anything, the weight of political support is on the side of the settlers, as is evident from a statement made in 1990 by the Congress (I) member of parliament from the islands, Manoranjan Bhakta: '... Job-seekers [settlers] who have come (to) the island are now serious contenders for allotment of house sites and agricultural land. Since the political system goes with the number, no political party is in a position to contradict their demands.'

The numbers, clearly, are working against the Jarawas. After all, 250 individuals do not count for much in the political system. For the Jarawas, however, this battle is not about political power; for them, it is literally a struggle for survival and against extinction. And if their land rights and other needs are not respected, they might very soon go down as another of the lost races of humankind.

Table 3. Population figures: A&N Islands and Andaman district

Year	A&N Islands Population	Decadal Growth Rate (%)	Andaman District Population	Decadal Growth Rate (%)
1901	24,649		18,138	
1911	26,459	7.34	17,641	–2.74
1921	27,086	2.37	17,814	0.98
1931	29,463	8.78	19,223	7.91
1941	33,768	14.6	21,316	10.89
1951	30,971	–8.28	18,962	–11.04
1961	63,548	105.19	48,985	158.33
1971	1,15,133	81.17	93,468	90.81
1981	1,88,741	63.93	1,58,287	69.35
1991	2,80,661	48.7	2,41,453	52.54
2001	3,56,265	12.79	3,14,239	30.14
2011	3,79,944	6.8	3,43,125	

Source: Census of India.

Table 4. Population of the Andaman tribal communities

	Great Andamanese	Onge	Jarawa	Sentinelese*	Total	Growth Rate
1901	625	672*	585*	117	1999	
1911	455	631*	114*	117	1317	−34.12
1921	209	346*	114*	117	786	−40.32
1931	90	250*	70*	50	460	−41.47
1941						
1951	23	150*	50*	50	273	−40.65
1961	19	129	500*	50	698	155.6
1971	24	112	250*	82	468	−32.95
1981	26	97	250*	100	473	1.01
1991	45	95	280*	100	520	9.93
2001	43	96	240	39	418	-19.61
2011	54	101	380	15		

*Estimates

Source: Census of India; see also, T.N. Pandit, *The Sentinelese*, Anthropological Survey of India, Calcutta: Seagull Books, 1990.

9

EMBRACING DISEASE[1]

30 September 1999

IN OCTOBER 1997, A new chapter began in the history of the Jarawas of the Andaman Islands. From being a hostile, uncontactable community, they took their first step out of their remote forest home to interact with the 'settlers', the people from mainland India who have settled along the forests that are home for the Jarawas.

In August 1999, less than two years since they first stepped out, the community was afflicted with an epidemic of measles and other infections. The first death was reported on 16 August 1999 itself: a young Jarawa woman named Madhuri had reportedly died due to acute broncho-pneumonial congestion. It took more than a month, however, for the news to come out when around thirty Jarawas were admitted to the G.B. Pant Hospital in Port Blair.

---

[1]While this particular piece was not previously published, a version with the same title appeared in *Down to Earth* dated 31 October 1999.

At the time, fifty-nine Jarawas of the estimated population of 250–300 were in hospital, suffering from measles, post-measles broncho-pneumonia infections and conjunctivitis. There is a possibility that pockets of infection still remain deep in the forest and more members of the tribe may get infected. 'It could well be the beginning of the end,' says Samir Acharya of the Society for Andaman and Nicobar Ecology (SANE), the first to bring the episode to light.

What is very worrying is that the history of the Andaman and Nicobar Islands is replete with the decimation of such tribal communities by diseases that they contracted after contact with the outside world. The most chilling example is that of the Great Andamanese. Hundreds of them died in epidemics of pneumonia in 1868, measles in 1877 and influenza in 1896. Combined with other factors like massacre by the colonial powers and the shrinkage of their forest habitat because of deforestation and settlements, they have been reduced from a population of a few thousand in the earlier part of the nineteenth century to less than fifty. Similar devastating outbreaks of measles have also been reported amongst tribal communities from around the world, the better known being that of the Nambikuara tribe from Brazil. Following an epidemic in 1945, the 10,000-strong community was reduced to less than 600 individuals.

The outbreak of the disease is an outcome of the policies and attempts of the administration to establish friendly contact with this 'hostile' community that had always shunned any interaction with the outside world. There still are opinions that the Jarawas should be assimilated into the modern world, but it is clear that it is exactly this contact with the outside world that is rapidly pushing them towards the brink.

Also, the most pressing question is what should be done now? The present medical treatment is only going to work in the immediate short term, and more concrete, sustainable steps are urgently needed if further outbreaks of even worse diseases like TB or hepatitis are to be avoided. One of the biggest vectors of outside intervention in the Jarawa territory is the Andaman Trunk Road (ATR) that connects Port Blair to the north of the islands. The ATR cuts through the heart of Jarawa territory and has been the single most significant factor in bringing in more outsiders close to the forest home of the Jarawas and to the Jarawas themselves. It has also encouraged encroachments into and exploitation of resources from within the Jarawa Reserve.

From the very beginning, environmental groups had been opposing the ATR, but their opinion was always ignored. 'Closing the ATR and putting an end to the indiscriminate interaction between the Jarawas and the settlers would appear to be the only way to save this ancient tribe,' says Acharya. According to him, the Directorate of Shipping has the resources (boats and manpower) to put in use as an alternative route between Port Blair and the Middle and North Andaman Islands. They have the wherewithal to take care of the entire load of passenger and cargo traffic that uses the ATR by the sea route, he says. This option needs to be urgently looked into and all support and resources that may be needed to make it operational should be immediately provided.

Also significant in this context is a writ petition filed recently by a local lawyer (though before the outbreak of the epidemic) asking for the rehabilitation of the Jarawa tribe (Chapters 10 and 11). This suggestion has been opposed by various Indian groups including SANE and Kalpavriksh. Reputed anthropologists from around the world, whose expert testimonies were compiled by the London-based Survival International and placed before the court in Port Blair via an intervention that was filed by SANE, too have argued that the Jarawas should be allowed to lead their traditional lives in the forests and any attempts to resettle or rehabilitate would only lead to disaster.

Discussing the health-related implications, James Woodburn of the Department of Anthropology, London School of Economics and Political Science, points out that when an isolated community with low population density (like the Jarawa) comes into contact with one of high density (like the settlers), the isolated group will become ill and many may die. Some of the diseases, measles for example, are density-dependent and do not take root in a population with low density. When an isolated community comes into contact with outsiders, because they have not acquired immunity in childhood, they are likely to be struck down by one illness after another. First they will be weakened, and if the next illness strikes during this period, people will die. 'It is not unusual' he warns, 'for 50 per cent or even more of the population to die in the first months or years of extensive contact.'

What is happening with the Jarawas today is proving to be exactly what had been predicted, and unless some steps to correct the situation are taken urgently, we could well be witnessing the pushing of another set of people into history.

10

DELIVERING THE JARAWAS

Frontline, 31 August 2001

COURT CASES INVOLVE COMPLEX processes, which sometimes take trajectories of their own and reach destinations not quite intended at the time of their initiation. In one such instance, an order that the Port Blair Circuit Bench of the Calcutta High Court[1] issued recently has turned out to be to the benefit of the indigenous Jarawa community of the Andaman Islands.

The case had its origins in an intriguing development that was noticed in October 1997 – a drastic change in the lifestyle and attitudes of the forest-dwelling Jarawas who were previously extremely hostile to outsiders. For reasons that are not yet clear, the Jarawas voluntarily came out from

---

[1] This is a case that is different and independent from the one in the Supreme Court discussed in Chapters 4, 5 and 6. There are, however, many overlaps in issues and implications of the different court orders.

their forest home to have peaceful interactions with the settler communities that live on the forest's edge.

Almost overnight, the hitherto feared and mysterious Jarawa became a subject of intense curiosity. People travelled to the margins of the forest to catch a glimpse of the tribe, and a small industry was created out of this. The impression gained ground that there was not enough food in the forests to support the community. Consignments of bananas, coconuts and papayas were sent in regularly and even air-dropped into the forests.

The end of the hostility of the Jarawas also saw the increased exploitation of resources from the Jarawa Reserve. Sand mining from the beaches on the western coast of the islands, poaching and removal of non-timber forest produce (NTFP) from the forest habitats increased. All this while, a few anthropologists, tribal rights activists and environmentalists kept arguing that outsiders had to be stopped from contacting the Jarawas, that providing them food was not the solution, and that the violation and exploitation of their forest habitats had to be stopped.

It was in this context that Shyamali Ganguly, a local lawyer, filed a writ petition before the Circuit Bench in May 1999. The petition, a classic example of a move undertaken with the right intentions but seeking the wrong solutions, asked for the administration's help to bring the Jarawas into the mainstream and improve their lives. The examples of the Great Andamanese and the Onge were held out to explain how this could be done. But surprisingly, the petitioner failed to notice that both these communities are on the verge of being wiped out, primarily because of attempts to 'civilize' and take them into the mainstream, made first by the British and later by the governments of independent India. The petition also asked that the Jarawas be relocated in another area, which would then be all theirs.

It was at this juncture that the Port Blair–based SANE intervened. 'What was asked for in the petition would have meant certain death for the Jarawas,' says Samir Acharya of SANE. SANE largely disagreed with the views of the petitioner, particularly in the matter of relocating the Jarawas, which it felt would be disastrous for the tribal community. Importantly, it requested the court to order the removal of all encroachments, camps and outposts from the Jarawa Reserve and to institute an inquiry into whether the Andaman Trunk Road (ATR) ought to be closed to traffic and alternative transport routes explored.

Help also came from Survival International, the London-based tribal rights organization, which contacted eight of the world's leading anthropologists. Their signed testimonies placed before the court unanimously said that the Jarawas should be allowed to maintain their traditional lifestyles in the forests and that any attempt to resettle or rehabilitate them would lead to disaster.

'Historic precedents involving the relocation and sedentarization of tribal peoples (particularly in island cultures) have often led to their complete destruction,' explained Mark Levene of the Department of History, University of Warwick, UK. Levene, a research scholar working in the area of genocide in the modern world, cited examples of such genocide in different parts of the world – of Tasmanians by the British settlers in the nineteenth century, of Chakmas from the Chittagong Hill Tracts (CHT) in South Asia, and of Amazonian tribes in Latin America.

Marcus Colchester of the Oxford-based Forest People's Programme argued that the relocation of the Jarawas could even be termed illegal under the International Labour Organization's (ILO) Convention 107 and Articles 7 and 10 of the United Nations Draft Declaration on the Rights of Indigenous Peoples, which prohibit 'the forcible removal of indigenous people from their lands ...' and 'any form of population transfer which may violate or undermine their rights ...'

On the issue of health, James Woodburn's observations regarding the implications of such contact on indigenous communities was like looking into a crystal ball. A couple of months later, in August 1999, an epidemic of measles hit the Jarawa tribe (Chapter 9). By the third week of October, 48 per cent of the estimated Jarawa population of 350 was suffering from disease and ill health. The affected people were treated mainly at the Primary Health Centre (PHC) in Kadamtala in the Middle Andamans and at the G.B. Pant Hospital in Port Blair. There were even reports that a couple of them had died in the forests. These reports could not be corroborated, but clearly the worst fears about their safety seemed to be coming true.

Fortunately, a team of doctors comprising Namita Ali, director of health services, Elizabeth Mathews, superintendent, G.B. Pant Hospital, and R.C. Kar, the medical officer in Kadamtala, did some commendable work, and not a single casualty was reported among those Jarawas who were admitted to the hospitals.

As for the court case, a six-member expert committee established by the court in February 2000 submitted its report six months later, in August. The committee had the chief judicial magistrate of Port Blair as its member secretary. Other members included two anthropologists, R.K. Bhattacharya and Kanchan Mukhopadhyay from the Anthropological Survey of India (ASI), and three doctors, Namita Ali, R.C. Kar and Anima Burman from Port Blair.

The committee pointed out that a preliminary study by the ASI had indicated that the forest had enough food resources to provide for the Jarawas and that there was no shortage of food; that they continue to be susceptible to many infectious diseases and that vigilance should not be slackened; that the maintenance of the ATR and procurement of wood for the purpose regularly degraded the forests; and that illegal fishing, poaching and removal of non-timber forest produce from the Jarawa Reserve were happening regularly. Many other conclusions of the committee were reflected in the order issued on 9 April in Port Blair by Justice Samaresh Banerjea and Justice Joytosh Banerjee. A detailed, sixty-page written order in the matter came from Calcutta more than six weeks later, on 28 May 2001.

The court directed the formation of another expert committee to look into the matter and gave it six months from the date of its formation to come up with a plan to deal with issues related to the Jarawas. The order also made a special reference to the 'Master Plan 1991–2021 for the Welfare of the Tribes of the A&N' prepared by S.A. Awaradi, former director, tribal welfare, in the Andaman and Nicobar administration. It indicated that the document should be taken into consideration while formulating the final policies. For the interim period, it had ordered a number of steps to be implemented on a war footing.

The court had directed the local administration to stop

poaching and intrusion into Jarawa territory and to prevent its further destruction by encroachment and deforestation. It ordered issuance of an 'appropriate notification clearly demarcating the Jarawa territory'. This would greatly help law enforcement, particularly in the detection and removal of encroachments. The court also ordered that penal measures be taken against encroachers and poachers, and importantly, against those among the police and civil authorities who are negligent in this regard.

Accepting the recommendations of the expert committee, the court directed that medical aid be given to the Jarawas only when they came out of the forest and sought it, and only to the extent necessary. It asked for periodic medical programmes for the Jarawas in their own territory and only to the extent necessary, so that they need not come out from the forests for such aid. Significantly, the court directed that until a policy on dealing with the Jarawas was finalized, no new construction or extension of existing construction should be undertaken in the Jarawa territory and no extension was to be made to the ATR.

The order has been welcomed by environmental and tribal rights activists familiar with the situation in the archipelago. It is considered a very positive order, and one with great potential for safeguarding the future of the tribal people here. Ensuring its implementation is the next big challenge, and a lot will depend on how and with how much sincerity this is done.

11

FAILING THE JARAWAS

Frontline, 5 December 2003

IN THE OVERALL ANALYSIS, the second expert committee
set up to look into the situation of the Jarawas, has failed
to deliver what was expected of it. In July 2001, the Port
Blair Circuit Bench of the Calcutta High Court had ordered
the setting up of this second expert committee (the first
one had been appointed in February 2000) in the wake
of a writ petition filed by a local lawyer in response to an
extraordinary situation arising in the islands (Chapters 8,
9 and 10).

The court had, in a follow up to the report of the first
expert committee, issued a detailed sixty-page order asking
the Ministry of Home Affairs (MHA) to constitute another
committee of experts that would a) spell out the reasons
that have caused the sudden change in the behaviour of the
Jarawas; and b) suggest remedial measures to enable the
government to formulate programmes to save the Jarawas

from extinction or the loss of their identity and culture by a merger with the vast humanity of the so-called civilized society.

In response, the MHA, reportedly after consultations with the A&N administration, appointed a seven-member committee with the chief administrator of the islands, Lt Governor N.N. Jha, as convener. Three of the other six members were from the local administration: Namita Ali, director of health services; S.A. Awaradi, director, tribal welfare; and Som Naidu, assistant commissioner, Mayabundar. The other three members were K.B. Saxena, former secretary, Ministry of Social Justice and Empowerment, Government of India; Indira Chakrabarty, dean and director of the Kolkata-based All India Institute of Hygiene and Public Health; and R.K. Bhattacharya, director of the Anthropological Survey of India (he had retired from service by the time the committee finalized and submitted the report to the court).

The members of the 'expert' committee were all government officials, either from the local administration or from the Central government. At the time of constituting the committee, the only person who could actually be considered to be outside the government framework was K.B. Saxena, although he too was a retired government employee. In this context, scepticism that there was little space for independent opinion and that the committee would not deliver much was certainly well placed.

Constituted in July 2001 with a wide-ranging mandate, the committee decided to study and survey the Jarawas and their forests through multidisciplinary teams which involved a cross section of disciplines and organizations, including the Anthropological Survey of India, the Botanical Survey of India (BSI), the Zoological Survey of India (ZSI), the All India

Institute of Hygiene and Public Health, the Andaman and Nicobar Forest Department and the Directorate of Health Services of the local administration. As expected, they went into a range of issues relating to the Jarawas such as their health, the status of their forest habitat, the availability of resources, their knowledge of the resources and the impact of the outside world. There was a steady traffic of experts and committees making its way to the Jarawa territory for more than a year.

Finally, in July 2003, two years after the committee was constituted, a 446-page report was submitted to the high court. It contained interesting and crucial new information about the Jarawas and understandably so, because it was for the first time in the history of the Jarawa community and of the A&N administration that such a detailed study was carried out.

For instance, the report has some fascinating information about the Jarawas' knowledge of their forests and the plants and animals found therein. It documents, for the first time, the Jarawa community's exhaustive understanding and use of their natural resources: they have knowledge of at least 150 plant and over 350 animal species, many of which are consumed as food or medicine, or are put to use for decorative purposes. The report also gives an idea of the way the Jarawas use the 700-odd sq. km of forest land that constitute the Jarawa Reserve;[1] how the community is divided into three main groups that are independent, but not isolated from each other; where their main camps are located in the forests; what

_____

[1] The area of the reserve was increased to a little more than 1,000 sq. km in 2004.

the resource availability with the changing seasons is; how the lives of the Jarawas themselves change with the seasons; and how the equations between the Jarawas and the settlers who surround their forests have been changing.

While the report does a good job here, the section that was supposed to contain the recommendations to formulate an action plan for the future of the Jarawas, delivers virtually nothing. The main chapter in the formal report, titled 'Summary and recommendations', has little that is of worth. What it makes clear is that there was no consensus in the committee on critical matters. Four members of the committee – S.A. Awaradi, Som Naidu, K.B. Saxena and R.K. Bhattacharya – have, in fact, submitted their independent notes, which are now part of the report before the court. Two of these notes, by Bhattacharya and Saxena respectively, constitute the most interesting and strongly persuasive parts of the report. Bhattacharya's two-page note deals exclusively with the contentious issue of the ATR. It says in no uncertain terms that the road should be shut down and that it would be a very important first gesture of goodwill to the extremely marginalized and vulnerable community.

The 100-odd-page note by Saxena is scathing in its analysis of the A&N administration's response to the situation and the problems of the Jarawa community. According to him, the fundamental problem was the committee itself. 'The composition of the committee,' he explains in his note, 'was flawed and precluded the possibility of meaningful discussion to attempt such an exercise. A majority of the members of the committee (four out of seven) were from the A&N administration and had obvious limitations in expressing their views freely and frankly. Three of them were subordinates to the fourth member [the convenor, who was the LG of the islands]. They hardly participated except when asked to respond to a situation/query by their head of organization. Their reactions were naturally tailored to safeguard their position.'

The Jarawas stand at a crossroads and any hope that the committee will signal to the administration the best course of action has been dashed. The court had also directed that within six months of submission of the report, the A&N administration should formulate a policy and a plan to deal with the situation of the Jarawa community. Policy formulation would have to be based on a series of seminars and open discussions that are to be organized by the government on the basis of the report.

The administration also had the mandate to issue public notifications in major newspapers and send invitation letters to anthropologists, sociologists, representatives of non-governmental organizations and any individual who has knowledge and experience in the matter concerned. They would then be at liberty to submit their own opinion and views, which have to be supported by cogent reasons and material, which will then have to be considered by the Central government while formulating the plan.

It is nearly two months since the report was submitted to the high court. However, none of the steps outlined by the court has been initiated. In fact, it was almost a month after the report was submitted to the court that it was made available to the public via the website of the Andaman and Nicobar administration. The administration needs to do much more to ensure that it meets its responsibility to the high court and the Jarawa community.

Box 6: Policy on the Jarawas

The 'Policy on the Jarawa Tribe of Andaman Islands' (see Appendix III for the full text of the policy), published in the *Andaman & Nicobar Gazette* on 21 December 2004, marked the culmination of a significant and interesting process in the Port Blair Circuit Bench of the Calcutta High Court.

It was triggered by a petition filed before the Circuit Bench in May 1999 by Shyamali Ganguly, a lawyer in Port Blair. The petitioner sought directions to the Andaman and Nicobar administration to improve the lives of the Jarawas and bring them into the mainstream, similar to what had been done with the Great Andamanese and the Onge, the other indigenous communities on the islands. It was clearly the wrong solution sought, because both these communities are today on the verge of being wiped out, primarily because of attempts to 'civilize' and 'mainstream' them. The trajectory of the case changed dramatically following an intervention by the Port Blair–based Society for Andaman and Nicobar Ecology (SANE), which argued that if the petitioner's demands were accepted, it would mean the end of the road for the Jarawas.

The court established an expert committee to go into the details of the matter as a first step in the formulation of a policy for the Jarawas. The expert committee submitted its report in July 2003. As directed by the high court, two seminars were organized, one in Kolkata in April 2004, and the other at Port Blair in May 2004, where experts, non-governmental organizations and individuals deliberated on issues relating to the Jarawas and their well-being.

The end product of the process was the formulation and finalization of the policy that has been acknowledged as a significantly progressive document, except on the closure of the Andaman Trunk Road, where the policy actually stands in violation of the Supreme Court's orders.

The objectives of the policy have been articulated as follows:

- to protect the Jarawas from the harmful effects of exposure and contact with the outside world while they are not physically, socially and culturally prepared for such interface;
- to preserve the social organization, mode of subsistence and cultural identity of the Jarawa community;
- to provide medical help to the Jarawas to reduce mortality and morbidity in case of their sudden affliction with diseases which their systems are unaccustomed to;
- to conserve the ecology and environment of the Jarawa Reserve territory and strengthen support systems in order to enable the Jarawas to pursue their traditional modes of subsistence and way of life;
- to sensitize settler communities around the Jarawas' habitat and personnel working for the protection and preservation of the Jarawas about the need to preserve this ancient community and to value their unique culture and lifestyle.

The policy further elaborates six strategies/guidelines to meet the above objectives under the broad categories of Protection of Cultural Identity, Protection of Natural Habitat, Protection of Health Status, Regulation of Traffic on Andaman Trunk Road, Codification of Jarawa Language and Institutional Arrangements.

The policy advocates 'maximum autonomy to the Jarawas with minimum and regulated intervention' by the government when needed. It says that the Jarawas will be allowed 'to develop according to their own genius' and that no attempts will be made either to mainstream them or rehabilitate them on other islands. Under the strategies for the protection of the natural habitat, the policy is clear that no encroachments will be tolerated in the Jarawa territory, that no natural resources will be extracted from the Jarawa Reserve even by government agencies, and that no attempt will be made 'to curtail, reduce or acquire land' from the notified Jarawa territory.

While there can be no denying that the policy is a significant and positive step forward, its real value can be gauged only when it is implemented. Reports and feedback from the ground, however, indicate that the policy is still only a piece of paper that reads and means well.

– *Frontline*, 9 September 2005

12

BECAUSE ANDAMAN'S FORESTS ARE JARAWA-INFESTED...

The Hindu, 19 January 2012

Infestation, in'fes•ta'tion: n. *the state of being invaded or overrun by pests or parasites.*

DO PEOPLE INHABIT THE lands and forests that they have been living in for thousands of years or do they infest them? The answer to this no-brainer of a question might well lie at the root of the problem being faced by the Jarawas in the Andaman Islands today. A recent video showing Jarawa women dancing on the Andaman Trunk Road, apparently for food, is just the latest manifestation of a malaise that is so deep that one might well argue that there is no hope for the Jarawa tribe.

In 1965, the Ministry of Rehabilitation, Government of India, published an important document related to the Andaman and Nicobar Islands titled 'The Report by the interdepartmental team on accelerated development programme for A&N Islands'. The contents of the report and their purpose were evident in the title itself – it laid out the road map for the development of these islands and set the stage for what was to happen over the decades that have followed.

This little known report running to 150-odd pages is remarkable for the insights it provides into the thinking and the mindset of the times. There is what one might call a shocker on every page of this document and here are just two samples of this:

Page 26: ... The Jarawas have been uniformly hostile to all outsiders with the result that about half the Middle Andaman is treated as a *Jarawa infested* [emphasis added] area which is difficult for any outsider to venture [into]... With the present road construction and the colonization of the forest fringes, friction has become more frequent, and no month passes without a case of attack by the Jarawas.

Page 69: The completion of the Great Andaman Trunk Road would go a long way to help in the extraction of forest produce ...

A nation that had just fought its way out of the ignominy of being a colony was well on the way to becoming a colonizer itself. And those that came in the way could only be pests or parasites infesting the forests that had valuable resources locked away from productive use.

It is also pertinent to note here that in 1957 itself, more than 1,000 sq. km of these 'Jarawa-infested' forests of South and Middle Andaman had already been declared protected as Jarawa Tribal Reserve under the provisions of the Andaman and Nicobar Protection of Aboriginal Tribes

Regulation (ANPATR), 1956. The 1965 report then was in complete violation, or was a result of complete ignorance of this legal protection to the Jarawa and the forests that they have inhabited for thousands of years.

The seeds that were sown then have bloomed into myriad noxious weeds today and if one knows this history, the latest video that has generated so much heat is not in the least bit surprising. Much space in the media, both print and electronic, has been occupied in the last few days by a range of claims and counter-claims – about the date of the video, about the police involvement in its making, the role of tour operators and about fixing blame and responsibility. A little-known fact that lies at the root of the issue has been all but forgotten – the existence of the Andaman Trunk Road, where this infamous video was shot about three years ago. The ATR that the 1965 report offered as a good way of extracting resources from the forests of the Jarawa had been ordered shut by a Supreme Court order of 2002 (see Chapters 5 and 6; Appendices I and II).

It has been a decade now and in what can only be called audacious defiance, the administration of this little Union territory has wilfully violated orders of the highest court of the land. A series of administrators have come and gone but contempt for the Supreme Court remains.

Whenever asked about the order, the administration has tried to hide behind technicalities of interpreting the court order and arguing that the court had never ordered the road shut in the first place. They forget that in March 2003, a few months after SC orders had been passed, they had themselves filed an affidavit with a plea to 'permit the use/movement through the Andaman Trunk Road'. If it was not ordered shut, why the plea to keep it open? A few months later, in July 2003, the Supreme Court–appointed Central Empowered Committee reiterated explicitly that court orders include those for the closure of the ATR in those parts where it runs through the forests of the Jarawa Tribal Reserve. The A&N administration has clearly violated the court's order both in letter and in spirit.

It is a spirit that was evocatively articulated by R.K. Bhattacharya, former director of the Anthropological Survey of India, in a report he submitted to the Calcutta High Court in 2004. 'The ATR,' he said, 'is like a public thoroughfare through a private courtyard ... In the whole of human history, we find that the dominant group for their own advantage has always won over the minorities, not always paying attention to the issue of ethics. Closure of the ATR would perhaps be the first gesture of goodwill on part of the dominant towards an acutely marginalized group almost on the verge of extinction.'

The video in all its perversity offers us another opportunity, when all others in the past have been brushed aside either due to ignorance or due to arrogance or sheer apathy. It is still not too late to make that 'gesture of goodwill' because otherwise, there will be many more such videos down the years and much worse will follow. Lessons from history are very clear on this. And it will hardly be any consolation that a few people will be left saying *we told you so*.

13

A ROAD STILL RUNS THROUGH IT

The Hindu, 5 Febraury 2013

ON 21 JANUARY 2013, the Supreme Court of India issued an order[1] banning tourists from using the ATR as it passes through the Jarawa Tribal Reserve. Ironically, the order was a direction to the Andaman and Nicobar (A&N) administration to implement its own notification of 2007 (Box 6).

The core idea of the initial notification (No.234/2007/F. No. 1-752/2007-TW) was to prevent 'any person other than a member of an aboriginal tribe' from indulging in any commercial and/or tourism activities in a buffer zone (BZ) of 5 kilometres from the boundaries of the Jarawa Reserve. The turn of events, however, is best highlighted by the fact

---

[1] This order is not related to the earlier story/case where the Supreme Court ordered the complete closure of the ATR. The order this article discusses came in a different context and in a different matter. (Also see Box 6 for a detailed chronology in this particular case.)

that during arguments in the court in July 2012, the Supreme Court was constrained to ask the A&N administration why it should not be held in contempt for non-implementation of the BZ notification that was its own creation. Something had obviously gone terribly wrong in the interim and one clue lies in trying to understand how the administration had sought to implement the notification.

There have been allegations that the BZ notification was brought in to target specific commercial entities, and circumstantial evidence too seems to point to this. Of the hundreds of big and small commercial enterprises in this buffer zone, for instance, only a handful were sent closure notices in the first three years after the notification came into force. In August 2009, the Calcutta High Court struck down the notification in response to an application filed by one of the resorts that had been shut down on account of the BZ notification. The administration went in appeal to the Supreme Court, which then asked explicitly for the full implementation of this buffer zone. It is here that the story begins to turn because the real implications started to show up.

Little, if any, thought had been put into the larger implications of the notification. There were a number of questions that the administration had not considered: What would it mean to restrict commercial activities in this 5-km buffer zone? How many villages of non-tribal settlers would this buffer zone include? How many people would be impacted? What would it mean for the livelihoods of thousands of these people if all commercial activities were to stop? Not surprisingly, there was and still is huge opposition to the buffer zone notification from the local population. The situation was beginning to get out of hand and that is when the administration tried to first dilute the provisions of its notification and then ignore the need for its implementation.

The issue of the ATR that lies at the heart of the court's recent orders has to be understood in this context. A part of the ATR has been used for many years now by tourists visiting the limestone caves and mud volcanoes on Baratang Island. Clearly, the use of ATR by tourists (a commercial activity) could not be permitted if the buffer zone notification was implemented in letter and spirit. The administration chose the 'don't see, don't hear, don't implement' way out of the logjam it had crafted for itself.

Importantly, the road has become, in recent years, the vector and the catalyst for a perverse kind of tourism, with tourists taking a ride here in the hope of catching a glimpse of the Jarawas who traditionally don't wear clothes. This whole thing exploded in early 2012 when videos were circulated by a British media house showing Jarawa women dancing on the ATR, allegedly, to get some food items from tourists. While all have not been convinced of the allegations, there was no doubt that the Jarawas were being compromised in different ways. The huge national and international uproar notwithstanding, the administration took what can be considered merely cosmetic steps.

It was repeatedly pointed out that the A&N administration was not just ignoring its own buffer zone notification, but that it was in far more serious contempt of an earlier Supreme Court order passed in a different case. In 2002, the court had ordered that the ATR be shut down completely in those parts where it runs through the Jarawa Tribal Reserve. Many commentators have noted that had the ATR been shut as per the 2002 order (Chapters 4 to 6; Appendices I and II), the current sorry state of affairs would never have come to pass. There would have been no traffic on the ATR, there would be no tourists, and a spectacle would not have been made of the Jarawas.

Ironically, the A&N administration was creating a buffer zone to secure the fringes of Jarawa territory at the same time as it was wilfully allowing its heart to be eaten away and destroyed. In an amendment brought in a few days ago on 17 January 2013, the lieutenant governor of the islands actually reduced the sea component of the Jarawa Reserve. The lip service being paid to the needs and welfare of the Jarawas is just that.

Tourism traffic on the ATR has now reportedly been stopped, but the sentiment and cynicism of the local population was captured neatly in a Facebook post by a Port Blair resident a day after the orders were issued: 'Take it from me,' it said, 'it would be business as usual.'[2]

---

[2] A subsequent order of the court in the matter, passed a few weeks later, allowed tourist traffic to resume on the ATR, albeit as part of convoys and with a strict list of dos and don'ts.

Box 7: The buffer zone notification: A chronology

October 2007: The A&N administration issues notification (No.234/2007/F.No. 1-752/2007-TW) under the Andaman and Nicobar Protection of Aboriginal Tribes Regulation (ANPATR, 1957) creating a buffer zone (BZ) with a 5-km radius around the reserve. The notification states that 'any person other than a member of an aboriginal tribe is prevented from entering the BZ for any commercial and/or tourism activities'.

November 2007: An order is issued by the administration to stop commercial activities in the BZ.

December 2007: Barefoot Resorts challenges the BZ notification in the court in Port Blair, alleging mala fide intention on part of the administration.

September 2008: The local court cancels the notification. The A&N administration goes for an appeal and the matter is referred to the Calcutta High Court.

August 2009: A division bench of the Calcutta High Court upholds the order of the local court. Notification remains cancelled.

March 2010: The A&N administration appeals to the Supreme Court (SLP No.12125 of 2010), which asks the A&N administration to give full effect to the BZ notification.

December 2010: The A&N administration sends out closure notices to a few commercial establishments. The notices are withdrawn in the face of protest by the local populations.

July 2012: A new BZ notification alters the meaning of the initial BZ, diluting its scope.

The Supreme Court directs the administration to take steps to bring the BZ notification into full effect immediately. During the hearing, the A&N administration is asked by the Supreme Court why it should not be considered in contempt for non-implemention of the notification.

17 January 2013: Another modidication of the BZ notification. Baratang and thirty-four revenue villages are excluded from the BZ. The notification also reduces the area of the Jarawa Tribal Reserve on the seaside.

21 January 2013: The Supreme Court asks for closure of tourist traffic on the ATR in keeping with the notification and also asks for an explanation as to why thirty-four villages should be excluded.

ENVIRONMENT, ECOLOGY AND DEVELOPMENT

14

TURTLE TALES

Frontline, 26 May 2000

ONE OF THE MOST eagerly awaited events in the wildlife calendar of the country is the mass nesting of tens of thousands of olive ridley sea turtles on the coasts of Odisha. This spectacular event, which has become immensely popular, draws a lot of media attention. However, in other parts of India, there are several nesting grounds of quite a few other turtle species that do not quite draw the attention they deserve. Perhaps the most significant of these 'neglected' areas are the remote islands of the Andaman and Nicobar in the Bay of Bengal.

The Odisha coast may be unmatched for the sheer numbers of the nesting ridleys, but the unique features of the turtle nesting grounds in the A&N Islands are the many species of turtles that nest here and the breathtaking beauty and landscape of the beaches and the islands themselves.

All the eight species of sea turtles that are found in the

oceans of the world are threatened and are listed in the *Red Data Book* of endangered animals of the International Union for the Conservation of Nature (IUCN). The Andaman and Nicobar Islands are considered the best nesting sites in India for three of these species: the giant leatherback, *Dermochelys coriacea*, the green sea turtle *Chelonia mydas*, and the hawksbill *Eretmochelys imbricata*. Additionally, the olive ridley *Lepdochelys olivacea* also nest here in substantial numbers.

Perhaps, the most comprehensive study of turtles in these islands is *The Status and Ecology of Sea Turtles in the Andaman and Nicobar Islands* by Satish Bhaskar of the Madras Crocodile Bank Trust (MCBT), published in 1993. Bhaskar's study, conducted over a decade and a half, has interesting and critical information on the turtles in the islands.

There are indications, however, that the turtle population in the islands is declining rapidly owing to a variety of factors – increased pollution of the ocean waters, death caused by turtles being ensnared in fishing nets, continued hunting of turtles for meat, destruction of turtle nests and large-scale destruction of beaches where turtles nest.

One of the most destructive influences are dogs, which were brought to the islands around 1860 by the British and which are now to be seen in many parts of the islands. Dogs regularly dig up turtle nests and destroy the eggs, pick up turtle hatchlings as they head back to the sea after hatching, harass the nesting adults, causing them extreme stress and on many occasions, even leading to the abandonment of the nest. The problem, reported from all over the islands, is reaching serious proportions.

Human population in the islands too has increased rapidly in the last few decades – from 50,000 in 1950 to an estimated 400,000 today – owing to large-scale immigration from mainland India. The expansion of human settlements has reduced and even eliminated nesting at several locations. Additionally, it has resulted in large-scale mining of sand from beaches for use in the construction industry. On the island, houses were traditionally built with timber but residents now opt for concrete structures, and the beaches are the only source of sand.

Despite the fact that beach sand, which is very fine and has high salt content, is unsuitable for use in construction and structures built with it have to undergo major repairs within a decade, it continues to be used. In 1995–96, about 70,000 to 80,000 cu.m of sand was mined from the beaches; the figures for 1997–98 were estimated to be about 157,000 cu.m. As a result, the beaches, many of which are important turtle nesting sites, have been destroyed.

A visit to the beaches around Port Blair offers telling evidence of erosion and ingress by the sea. Narrow strips of sand are all that remain and several trees lie toppled over the shore. The scene is much the same at the beaches at Corbyn's Cove, Wandoor and Chidiyatapu, all of which are less than an hour's drive from Port Blair. In these sites, there is no more sand to be mined and the operations have moved further afield to more remote beaches.

In the tiny settlement of Shoal Bay 19 (SB19), about 20 km north of Port Blair, sand mining over the last decade has systematically destroyed the beach, which was a turtle nesting site. Seawater now moves further into the settlement areas and has caused extensive damage to the paddy crop.

In a few other areas, the destruction of the beaches has led to increased erosion and ruined plantation crops such as coconut and areca, and roads have also been washed away in some places.

Such destruction of beaches poses a serious threat to turtles in the islands. The beaches at Corbyn's Cove, Wandoor, Chidiyatapu and SB19 were important turtle nesting sites. Rev. Henry Corbyn (after whom the beach is named) had observed in 1860 that there was 'a large sandy beach' at the site; today, Corbyn's Cove is promoted as a tourist spot but little of the turtle nesting habitat remains.

The case of the Cuthbert Bay Turtle Sanctuary in Middle Andaman, one of the more important turtle nesting sites in the islands, is somewhat ironic. On the one hand, it is promoted as a tourist destination for its scenic beauty and nesting turtles, while on the other, a part of this beach has been handed over to contractors for sand mining, which affects the turtles and defeats the very purpose of establishing the sanctuary and promoting tourism. The establishment of a fisherman's colony here and the proliferation of dogs have added to the problem.

The beach at Wandoor, on the boundary of what is now the Mahatma Gandhi Marine National Park, was heavily mined for sand about fifteen years ago. Even the mangroves that protected the land from sea erosion were indiscriminately destroyed. Today, little of the beach remains. Sea erosion has increased and now threatens the road that runs along the waterfront. This is a common enough experience in the islands and so is the response: people recently constructed a 'sea retaining wall' to check erosion – a function that was hitherto provided for free by the beach sand and the mangroves. Ironically, this wall too is a concrete structure, built using sand mined from some other beach nearby.

The threat to the turtles from all these factors must be dealt with urgently. Solutions are needed on many fronts: an alternative medium for construction must be conceived; the dog menace must be controlled; and measures must be initiated to prevent the killing of turtles by the islanders, particularly the fisherfolk. There have in recent times been some positive moves in this direction. The Andaman Public Works Division, the largest consumer of beach sand, and the Tourism Department have indicated a willingness to minimize the use of sand in their construction work and, where possible, to opt for alternative construction materials such as timber, which is abundantly available. Non-governmental organizations (NGOs) such as ANET, SANE and Kalpavriksh have been collaborating with the Directorate of Education in an attempt to spread environmental awareness and sensitivity among the people of the islands.

The needs of wildlife conservation and those of human communities have always appeared to be in conflict. In the Andaman and Nicobar Islands, however, the opposite is proving to be true: the destruction of the beaches, which the turtles use for nesting, threatens the survival of one of nature's most magnificent creatures. But the human communities that depend directly on this environment are also being forced to pay a heavy price, both ecological and economic. Sensible conservation policies must be evolved in order to ensure that for once there will be no losers, only winners.

Box 8: Marine turtles: A brief introduction

Marine turtles lead a completely aquatic existence and, excepting the female when laying eggs, they do not come ashore once they reach the sea from the sands under which they hatched. All have paddle-shaped limbs. The longer front limbs are used for swimming, being moved through water in a manner comparable to the wing beats of a bird. The head and limbs cannot be retracted into the shell. In food habits, they may be herbivorous, carnivorous or omnivorous. Turtles are known to man from their habit of coming ashore to bury their eggs under the sands on the seashore, a habit recorded as early as the fourth century AD in Tamil literature. Marine turtles are mainly tropical in distribution but some species occasionally enter temperate seas.

Green sea turtle: Adults can attain a carapace length of over a metre and weight up to 150 kg. The hatchling is dark blue-black in colour whereas the adults are olive green or brown above, with spots or blotches or streaks of brown or black. The female is usually more richly pigmented than the male. The turtle is herbivorous when adult and feeds on marine algae and sea grasses.

Leatherback turtle: The largest of the sea turtles, it can grow up to about 1.8 m in length and weigh up to 600 kg. They live mainly on jellyfish and are believed to be deep-sea feeders.

Olive ridley turtle: These attain a carapace length of about a metre. The adult turtle is olive brown above and yellowish below, and is an omnivorous feeder. It is widely distributed in the tropics of the Indo-Pacific and the East Atlantic, and is the commonest turtle found along Indian coasts.

Hawksbill turtle: Grows up to a size of about a metre, and is distinguished by the strongly overlapping shields of the carapace. The adult is marbled, yellow-and-dark-brown above. This turtle is also omnivorous, but is inclined to be largely carnivorous, feeding on sponges, other invertebrates and also fish. The flesh of the turtle is said to be poisonous in certain seasons and instances of death from eating turtle flesh are attributed to this species.

Some threats to marine turtles: Huge trade in turtle eggs and meat continues across the world and the fishing and trawling industry too has inflicted a heavy toll on marine turtles. Amongst the worst sufferers have been the olive ridleys. Indraneil Das, chairperson of the IUCN South Asian Reptile and Amphibian Specialist Group, estimates that 30,000 ridleys were once consumed annually in the state of Kerala alone. More recently, in 1998, an equal number of dead ridleys were washed on to the Odisha coast; the turtles had drowned after being ensnared in trawling nets. The fat, meat and cartilage of the green sea turtle are used to make soup and other delicacies and its flippers are hacked to make shoes for protection against sharp coral. Parts of the hawksbill turtle are used to make turtle shell products such as combs, cigar cases, boxes and various ornaments. Large numbers of these species continue to be slaughtered for these purposes. In Tamil Nadu, oil is extracted from the carapace of the giant leatherback which is applied on wooden boats to prevent leaks. The oil is also believed to have medicinal properties, principally in the cure of asthma.

[Based on information mainly taken from J.C. Daniel, *The Book of Indian Reptiles and Amphibians*, New Delhi: Oxford University Press and Mumbai: Bombay Natural History Society (BNHS), 2002]

15

ECOLOGICAL TREASURES ... UNLIMITED

The Hindu, 7 July 2002

FOR A FIELD BIOLOGIST of any kind, be it marine, herpetological or botanical, the Andaman and Nicobar Islands are the ecological equivalents of the well-known 'magician's hat'. Put in a little effort, some resources and time, and out comes a fascinating 'rabbit'. So much so that every time there is a field study or survey in the islands, some new information becomes available.

Two recent surveys in the islands, one regarding corals and another regarding the giant leatherback turtle prove just that. Coming in quick succession in the last few months, both the findings are being considered as being globally significant. In April 2001, an international team comprising Indian, British and Australian scientists conducted a ten-day remote sensing and rapid survey-based study of the coral reefs of the Andaman Islands. Thirteen sites were surveyed as part of this joint project of the Government of India (GoI) and the United Nations Development Programme – Global Environment Facility (UNDP-GEF). The surveys recorded 197 species of coral, of which 111 were new finds for the A&N. It is indicative of how little these islands have been studied and of the actual richness of the diversity here. One species of coral was a new find for science and another one, found commonly during the dives, had earlier been reported only from the Philippines. The potential of what lies ahead is evident from the fact that this discovery came from only ten days of work in thirteen Andaman sites. The Nicobar Islands, which are likely to spring many surprises, were not looked at, at all.

It is being suggested that the total number of coral species in these islands could be around 400. This would then compare to the richness of the coral triangle, the area of the greatest marine diversity on earth, comprising the Philippines, Indonesia and Papua New Guinea. The A&N lie just north-west of this coral triangle and at 400 species, would be supporting about 80 per cent of the diversity found in the coral triangle.

The study reported that the reefs in the Andamans were more diverse than expected and less impacted than had been feared by other scientists working within the Indian Ocean region. A surprising find was that the reefs were hardly affected by coral bleaching that had devastated coral reef systems worldwide in 1998. Possible infestation by the crown-of-thorns starfish, another threat, was also non-existent. The conclusions, as the authors point out, are extremely significant. Not only are the coral reefs here globally significant in terms of reef diversity, their extremely healthy status may prove the area to be an important stronghold for corals in the Indian Ocean region and provide a reliable source for natural seeding and rehabilitation of other impacted coral reefs here.

Good coral populations indicate a healthy marine system, which in turn is very critical for other species that inhabit the oceans, sea turtles for example. The other significant finding is regarding the nesting populations in the islands of the giant leatherback turtle (*Dermochelys coriacea*), the largest marine reptile. Conducted by ANET, the study is part of the ongoing GoI–UNDP Sea Turtle Project in the country. The first authenticated report of the giant leatherback nesting in the islands was made as recently as 1978, when Satish Bhaskar of MCBT conducted his turtle surveys here. MCBT and ANET continued with detailed and more intensive surveys at regular intervals, the latest of which was completed in 2001.

Writing in the recent issue of the sea turtle conservation newsletter, *Kachhapa*, Harry Andrews of ANET and Kartik Shanker of the Wildlife Institute of India (WII), report that ' ... the total population (based on the latest surveys) of adult female leatherbacks that use the beaches in these islands for nesting exceeds 1,000 individuals'. Only three other colonies in the world are reported to have more than 1,000 individuals, clearly indicating that this island group is very critical for the long-term survival of this species. The status of the leatherback has, in fact, been recently changed from endangered to critically endangered. The threats to the turtles in the A&N are manifold. A pertinent example comes from Great Nicobar Island, the most important of the leatherback nesting sites in the A&N. During the 2000–01 nesting season, a staggering 40 per cent of the nesting leatherbacks had boat propeller cuts on their flippers, necks and carapaces, thanks mostly to the heavy ship and boat traffic from South-East Asia that transits just south of the Nicobars. Andrews further reports that between 1981 and 2000, at least twenty-one beaches (including five in Great Nicobar itself) that were regularly used by different species of sea turtles, have been completely mined away for the booming construction industry in the islands. It has also been estimated that feral dogs predate nearly 70 per cent of the eggs and hatchlings of the sea turtles in these islands. Given this scenario, the chances of survival of these and other species of turtles seem rather bleak.

Some direction and hope has, in fact, come from an unexpected source. The Supreme Court recently passed landmark orders for the conservation and protection of these islands (see Chapters 5 and 6; Appendices I and II). As a consequence, tree felling in the islands has been reduced substantially, sand mining from the beaches of the islands is to be reduced over the next few years, forest encroachments are being removed, and steps are being initiated to limit the immigration of people from mainland India. Though sand mining needs to be reduced much faster and far more drastically, the court order has initiated the first step in the right direction.

The court order should help the coral reefs too. A 1989 study by the Indian National Trust for Art and Cultural Heritage titled 'An investigation into the effects of siltation, logging, blasting and other human-derived damage to the coral islands in the Andaman and Nicobar Islands' – has reported that the maximum percentage of dead coral was found around the jetty at Hut Bay, the main Little Andaman Island town. The relative abundance of live coral here was reported to be only about 12 per cent. The reasons were clear. There was large-scale logging and a huge timber yard in the vicinity. Soil erosion was high and the seawater was dark and muddy, preventing light penetration and affecting the growth of corals. Mud accumulation on the seabed was found to be very high and silt accumulation was also seen on the corals themselves. Many such interesting and significant studies have never been considered by the bureaucrats and planners while planning the future of the islands. That this knowledge should become part of the information base when decisions are taken is very important. The survival of the biological wealth of the islands and also of the human communities that live here will critically depend on that.

The rabbits too will keep coming out!

Box 9: Endemicity in the islands

Of special importance while discussing the ecological profile of these islands is the high level of endemism. Overall, 9 per cent of the fauna is endemic: 40 per cent of the 244 species and subspecies in the case of birds and 60 per cent of the fifty-eight species of mammals. The A&N Islands support a significant diversity of reptiles and amphibians, also with a high level of endemism. Currently, seven amphibians and sixteen reptile species are considered endemic to the Andamans and two amphibians and fifteen reptiles are endemic to the Nicobars.

Representing 700 genera and belonging to 140 families, about 14 per cent of the angiosperm species are endemic to the islands. Among the non-endemic angiosperms, about 40 per cent are not found on mainland India, but have only extra-Indian distribution in South-East Asia. The butterfly diversity and endemism is also high; reported to be over 50 per cent of the 214 species and 236 subspecies that are found here.

The endemism is due to the isolation of the islands from mainland Asia. Thus, considering the size and area of the islands, loss of habitat leading to extinctions will have far greater consequences in terms of the loss of genetic diversity than in comparable areas elsewhere. A rough calculation using the island biogeography theory indicates that with the forest area down to 86 per cent of what it used to be, about 4.5 per cent of species may have already been lost.

Source: *The Andaman and Nicobar Islands Biodiversity Strategy and Action Plan*, Port Blair: Andaman and Nicobar Islands Environmental Team, 2003.

16

AN EXOTIC PROBLEM

Sanctuary Asia, September 2003

'IRONIC' IS THE TERM that comes to mind. A wildlife sanctuary protecting an animal that should not be there in the first place! Anywhere else in the country, a sanctuary protecting the increasingly threatened Asian elephant would be a welcome step. In the 131-sq. km Interview Island Sanctuary in the northern part of the Andaman Islands, however, it is a completely different story. How this situation came about is extremely interesting, the origins of which lie in the islands' seemingly unrelated logging and timber extraction industry. Elephants played a critical role in these operations, which were stopped only recently following orders of the Supreme Court.

Nearly five decades ago, a private enterprise from Kolkata, P.C. Ray & Co., was granted a contract for timber extraction from Interview Island. In the early 1960s, the company went bankrupt and had to withdraw. Unable to transport the elephants back, forty-odd animals were let loose on the uninhabited island. They turned feral and actually flourished.

So what is the problem, you might ask. A serious one going by research done, first in 1994, by the Coimbatore-based Salim Ali Centre for Ornithology and Natural History (SACON) and then in 2002, by the Andaman and Nicobar Islands Environmental Team (ANET). The basic problem lies in the fact that elephants and many other creatures, including the spotted deer, cat, dog and squirrel (all mammals), birds like the common crow, common myna and the peafowl and other creatures such as the giant African snail that are found on the islands today do not actually belong here. They are alien species introduced into the islands via ill-advised human intervention.

'Alterations induced by alien species can disturb the structure and functioning of the invaded systems with profound impacts,' says R.S. Rana, former director of the New Delhi–based National Bureau of Plant Genetic Resources. His recent paper, 'Alien Invasive Species and Biodiversity: Indian Perspective', prepared for the National Biodiversity Strategy and Action Plan, further adds: '... while all continental areas have suffered from biological alien invasions, the problem is particularly acute on islands and the ecological cost is the irretrievable loss of native species and ecosystems.'

'The dynamics of introduced species on island systems like the Andaman and Nicobar,' explains Rauf Ali who conducted the study on behalf of ANET, 'have aroused a lot of concern worldwide. They have a great impact on the vegetation patterns of the areas where they occur and island ecosystems are particularly vulnerable.' Introduction of exotics, in fact, may prove more damaging to the local environment than degradation and fragmentation of habitats. He also points out that the introduction of grazing animals such as the elephant or deer can lead to the extinction of local or endemic species (not found anywhere else in the world) and this has a disproportionately large impact on islands.

Experiences from around the world have, in fact, also shown that continental species rapidly replace native island residents. This is explained by the fact that a greater number of aggressive species evolve simultaneously on continents. These exert a high selection pressure on the other species so that in the long run, each evolves into a species with greater competitive ability.

The 1994 study on Interview Island by N. Sivaganesan and Ajith Kumar found that the elephant population had risen from around forty to seventy-one and that this had led to a significant impact on the native vegetation. Some plant species, particularly cane, bamboo and pandanus were reported to be in decline. The study concluded that the elephants were a major threat to native plant species. The habitat changes induced by the elephants could possibly result in the loss of microhabitats to the detriment of species such as the king cobra and the water monitor lizard.

The 2002 ANET study found that the elephant population had declined to half since the last study and now stood at around thirty-five. Shortage of food was considered to be the major reason for this decline, though poaching and disease may well have been factors. The study, in fact, confirmed that cane, bamboo and pandanus, favoured elephant foods, were now virtually absent, except on very steep and inaccessible rocky slopes. There was also major damage caused by debarking trees, mainly the smaller ones having a diameter in the 10–40 cm range. Across the island, all such trees would eventually die. There was also extensive soil erosion and the forest understorey was fast vanishing, indicating a threat to the long-term survival of the forest itself.

The situation on Interview Island is compounded by the presence of another introduced and highly prolific herbivore, the spotted deer. These deer were the subject of another study published in 2002 by Bandana Aul of the Salim Ali School of Ecology and Environmental Sciences, Puducherry. The study attempted to quantify the damage caused by spotted deer to the rate of natural regeneration in small island ecosystems such as the Andamans (there are no deer populations in the Nicobar group of islands).

Though not based in Interview Island, the results can be applied here, as well as to the other islands that harbour 'foreign' deer populations. The study concludes that 'since chital browse extensively on seedlings, the high densities of chital have affected the natural regeneration of forests in the Andaman Islands,' and that, 'there is an urgent need to start reducing the population'. It goes on to suggest that hunting licences be issued and that deer ranching as practised by New Zealand be permitted. ANET too suggests that the elephants on Interview Island be removed urgently 'to preserve this unique ecosystem'. No one is likely to disagree with this, but it is not clear how this goal should be achieved.

The urgency is evident from the magnitude of the problem and its potential consequences. It can be extremely significant in terms of biodiversity loss. Perhaps 14 per cent of the flora of the Andaman Islands is endemic. The rich fauna of the islands is dependent on the flora. Over 40 per cent of the bird life, 60 per cent of mammals and 32 per cent of reptiles are endemic to the Andaman and Nicobar Islands and we could lose many of these if a solution is not quickly found.

In this context, the detailed orders that the Supreme Court issued recently are important. One of them dealt with the issue of exotics, while another has led to a cessation of timber operations on the islands. This, of course, is a vital step for the protection of these rich and unique rainforests, but there is concern about the fate of the many elephants that are owned by the Forest Department and private sawmill owners. Will they, like the animals left behind by P.C. Ray & Co., turn feral and therefore destructive? Under no circumstances must this be allowed to happen. They must be returned to mainland India, and it seems traders from the mainland have indicated their willingness to bear the cost of such transport.

But getting the elephants off Interview Island is not going to be easy. They are far from meek and will probably need a veritable army of experts. To date, however, no one seems to have even thought of this problem, leave alone the plan that will be needed for the evacuation.

Box 10: The giant African snail

The possible consequence of introducing exotic species into an island system is perhaps best illustrated by the example of the giant African snail *Achatina fulica*. These snails were first introduced into the A&N Islands by the Japanese in the early 1940s, presumably as a protein supplement to their diet. During the last six decades, they have spread to all the major islands from North Andaman to Great Nicobar and have become a serious threat to vegetable crops. The attempted solution, the introduction of two predatory snails in the 1960s as biological control agents for the giant African snail, only appears to have compounded the problem. From the situation in the islands today, it is clear that the giant African snail continues to proliferate beyond control.

It is feared that the new introductions may actually have had a negative impact on other snail species in the islands. One of the introduced predatory snails, *Euglandia rosea* has proved to be disastrous for the snail fauna in other island systems where it was introduced. In Hawaii, where it was introduced to control the giant African snail, it has brought about the extinction of half of the forty-four species of the Hawaiian *Achatinelia* snails. On the island of Mooera in French Polynesia too, *Euglandia rosea* has driven to extinction seven species of endemic snails that were found there. This led the IUCN to pass a resolution at the seventeenth session of its General Assembly in Costa Rica in 1988, recommending that carnivorous snails should not be introduced in areas with an endemic snail population.

It is significant in this context that seventy-five of the eighty-five species of snails found in the A&N Islands are endemic. Little is known of their current status and we don't know how many may have gone extinct, either.

Box 11: Exotics that could not make it

It is pertinent to mention here that not all animals that arrive in, or are introduced to a new place, manage to survive. Many perish in the struggle for existence. The A&N Islands have had their share of introduced species that have failed to survive:

Mammals: Spotted deer and sambar were introduced to the island of Camorta in the Nicobar group in 1870. Spotted deer in particular have multiplied extensively in the Andaman Islands and have reached pest proportions in absence of any natural predators. However, they did not survive in Camorta, and neither did the sambar. Some sambar and two leopards were also introduced in the Middle and South Andaman Islands in the 1950s, but have not been seen since.

Birds: Of the many birds that have, over a period of time, been introduced to these islands, some have proliferated and could become a serious threat to native species. These include the common crow, peafowl, house sparrow, grey partridge and the common myna. The current status of the many others that were introduced is not known, but presumably they failed to establish themselves in the islands. These include the spot-billed duck, common quail, comb duck, and the open-bill stork, all of which were introduced in 1964.

The other rather interesting case is that of the barn owl, six pairs of which were brought to the islands from Tamil Nadu in 1991. The plan was to introduce them in the red oil palm (another exotic!) plantation in Little Andaman with the aim of controlling the spiralling rodent population. There was, however, strong opposition to this introduction, led by SANE. Consequently, the birds were sent back to the mainland within a week.

Insects: A number of insects of economic importance have been deliberately introduced in the islands since the 1960s. These include the lac insect in 1964–65, the honeybee *Apis cerana* in 1964, the pollinating weevil in 1986 and the silk moth in 1987. Today, naturalized populations of only the honeybee and the pollinating weevil can be seen in some parts of the Andamans. The others have failed to survive.

[These notes are based on information from P. Mohanraj, K. Veenakumari and A.K. Bandopadhyay, *Perilous Aliens*, Port Blair: Central Agricultural Research Institute, 1999.]

17

EXTINCTION BY PROTECTION

Indian Birds, 2009

THE PATH TO HELL, for humans, it is said, is paved with good intentions. For a little bird in the Andaman and Nicobar Islands, the edible-nest swiftlet *Collacalia fuciphaga*, the path to extinction, it would seem, too has been paved with similar good intentions.

Being listed in Schedule I of the Wild Life (Protection) Act, 1972 (WLPA), is the ultimate recognition of the endangered status of any creature in India. It also means that the highest degree of protection will be accorded to the species, and this is exactly what has happened in the case of the edible-nest swiftlet too. Herein lies the ultimate paradox and the seeds, probably, of an unfolding tragedy.

At the crux of the matter is the nest of the bird that is made entirely of its own saliva. The final product is a beautiful white 'half-cup', roughly 6 cm across with an average weight of 10 gm. This is indeed a fascinating biological quirk, but one for which the bird has had to pay a heavy price. Since the sixteenth century, when the nest of the bird is reported to have become an important part of Chinese cuisine and pharmacy, it has been heavily exploited across its range. While there is little modern scientific evaluation or validation of the efficacy or efficiency of the nest, consumption has been immense.

A *TRAFFIC International* publication of 1994 estimated that about nine million nests, weighing nearly 76 tonnes, were being imported into China annually. Not surprisingly then, the wholly edible white nest was, and continues to be, one of the world's most expensive animal products, pegged sometime back at US $2,620–4,060 per kg in retail markets in South-East Asian countries.

It is well known that a part of the international trade was being fed by nests extracted in the Andaman and Nicobar Islands, but authentic information started coming in only in 1995, when the first studies were initiated by ornithologist Ravi Sankaran of SACON. He initiated a laborious and painstaking process of locating the nesting sites and enumerating the nests and birds. Detailed surveys were conducted on the islands between March 1995 and early 1997, where he visited a total of 385 caves. The outcome were two pioneering reports. The first, published in 1995, dealt with the Nicobars and the second, in 1998, presented a complete picture of the situation in the entire archipelago.

Sankaran's studies estimated that about 6,700 breeding pairs constituted the total breeding population on the islands. He reported that at least 94 per cent of the caves were being exploited for the bird's nest, and that less than 1 per cent of the breeding population was being allowed to successfully fledge as the nests were being harvested for the market before the nesting could be completed. Sankaran estimated that the bird had experienced a whopping 80 per cent decline in its population in the islands, placing it in the critically threatened category (IUCN criteria A1c). This was primarily due to indiscriminate and unrestricted nest collection from the wild. Sankaran warned that if this was not dealt with urgently, the bird would soon be extinct in the Andaman and Nicobar Islands.

He initially advocated strict protection, but changed his stand when he realized that protection, in the conventional sense, would not work. He also learnt of the ingenious house-ranching methods developed by the Indonesians for managing the swiftlets. It was estimated that nearly 65,000 kg of nests were being produced in Indonesia annually from colonies of the edible-nest swiftlet that reside within human habitation: a total of 5.5 million birds and their nests, in houses and rooms of human habitations, optimally managed by humans. 'Thus, while swiftlet populations in caves will continue to decline, or become extinct, due to collection pressures,' Sankaran concluded, 'the species will survive because there are hundreds of thousands of birds that reside within human habitation, all optimally managed.'

Nest collectors, he started to advocate, would have to be empowered to harvest nests within the rigid framework of strictly scientific harvesting regimes. This would have to be complemented in the 'Indonesian way', with a realistic long-term strategy that would include both in situ conservation programmes as well as those away from the original place, i.e., house ranching, both based on the economic importance of the species and using this importance to organize local communities to conserve the species.

In 1999, his recommendation took the form of an innovative initiative that was launched jointly by the Wildlife Circle of the Department of Environment and Forests, Andaman and Nicobar Islands, and SACON. The final aim of the initiative was to ensure protection of the nests in the wild so that eggs would be available for the house ranching component, away from the original location. The project took off well. Protection accorded to twenty-eight caves in the Challis Ek cave complex in North Andaman Island, and one cave on Interview Island Wildlife Sanctuary, saw over 3,000 chicks being fledged, a growth of over 25 per cent in the population of the swiftlets at these sites. A team of local people, who were earlier nest collectors, were now being motivated towards protection, and subsequently, sustainable harvesting.

Just as the first phase was taking off, the law came into force, and in October 2003 the edible-nest swiftlet was put onto Schedule I of the Wild Life Act. This meant that there could be no activity that involved use of, or trade in, the nest of the bird – the primary premise on which Sankaran's initiative had been based. The entire project received a setback and, in spite of continued efforts over the years to have the swiftlet removed from Schedule I, it continues to be listed.[1]

---

[1] The bird was finally moved out of the Schedule I of the WLPA in 2009 ('Selling bird's nest soup to save this bird: there's a change in law,' http://www.indianexpress.com/news/selling-birds-nest-soup-to-save-this-bird-theres-a-change-in-law/503342/0 Tuesday, 18 August 2009.) Efforts for the conservation of the bird in the islands continue but the house-ranching project has still not taken off in the way it had been initially planned and hoped for.

Admittedly, there are genuine concerns about the delisting of a species and the implications of an act of this kind. The biggest fear is of setting a precedent that could be misused by vested interests. In this case, however, the recommendations are based on solid, detailed and pioneering scientific studies of nearly a decade and are, in turn, backed with a wealth of international information and experience. 'It's more like apiculture,' is Sankaran's argument, 'where bees are reared for their honey. House ranching of swiftlets cannot be likened to the farming of animals for skin or meat.'

The implication of not delisting the bird is that the conservation initiative is bound to fail, while harvesting from the wild would continue unabated. The consequences of this could be the local extinction of the bird in the Andaman and Nicobar Islands – a predicament that was summed up with stunning simplicity by J.C. Daniel of BNHS. Speaking during the concluding session of the international seminar to commemorate the centenary of the *Journal of the Bombay Natural History Society* in Mumbai in November 2003, he spoke of the fate of the edible-nest swiftlet if corrective action was not taken at the earliest: extinction by protection – the ultimate oxymoron.

18

THE NEW MILLENNIUM TAMASHA

The Hindu, 19 September 1999

THE ROYAL GREENWICH OBSERVATORY had announced a few years ago that the first sunrise of the new millennium would be visible from the island of Katchal in the Nicobar group of islands in the Bay of Bengal. The recent few months have seen the tourism industry and the A&N administration in a tizzy as they went about planning a huge millennium tamasha here. Efforts were on to get more than 20,000 tourists (largely foreigners) to the tiny and remote island of Katchal, which was advertised as the only place in the world where the first sunrise of the millennium will be visible.

It appeared to be the perfect situation for a huge tourism event – an exotic, remote island, an occasion that will never come again, and a government eager and willing to lay out the red carpet. However, the entire event came to be seriously questioned and opposed by a number of environmental groups from across the country as there were serious flaws. The opposition was strong and sustained and eventually the administration had to respond. In a secretary-level meeting held in Port Blair in early August 1999, a decision was taken to scale down the plan substantially.

The campaign that was coordinated by SANE was based on detailed research and solid facts. The very fact that Katchal was being promoted as the *only place* where the *first sunrise of the new millennium* will be visible is incorrect. A clarification issued by experts of the internationally renowned, Pune-based Inter-University Centre for Astronomy and Astrophysics (IUCAA) categorically asserted that these claims were preposterous and that there were at least two falsehoods that were being perpetrated – one that the new millennium begins on 1 January 2000, and the other that Katchal is the only place where the sunrise will be visible.

Experts all over the world, and this includes the United States Naval Observatories, the National Bureau of Standards and Technology of the US and the Royal Greenwich Observatory, England (before its demise in 1998) have accepted and adopted 1 January 2001 (and not 2000) as the beginning of the new millennium. The explanation for this is rather simple. There was no zero year and we actually began this calendar with the year 1. Accordingly, the first year was completed at the end of year 1, the first century at the end of year 100, the first millennium at the end of year 1000 and this, the second millennium, at the end of year 2000. Therefore, 1 January 2000 is only the first day of the last year of this millennium and not the beginning of the new one. The Y2K problem seems to have struck here as well, but in an entirely different way.

The second issue is of the site where this first sunrise would be visible. From a technical point of view, the issue of the first sunrise is not as simple as it initially seems. The US Naval Observatory in its document titled 'First Sunrise of the New Millennium' discusses some of these issues in detail: '... It is important to realize that on *any* 1 January, the sun is continuously above the horizon across most of Antarctica.' So, very simply put, the place where the first sunrise of the new millennium will be seen is Antarctica. However, beyond this, the question becomes more involved. Does the new day begin at local midnight, in the time defined by the local jurisdiction? Or, does it begin at midnight on the meridian of Greenwich in England, which is the zero longitude meridian, i.e., 0 hours GMT (Greenwich Mean Time) also known as 0 hours UT (Universal Time)?

Significantly, the paper states that at 0 hours UT, which is generally taken to be the start of a new day, the sun is rising simultaneously along an arc that runs 650 km east of Kerguelen Island in the Indian Ocean to about 640 km east of Amsterdam Island, through the Nicobar Islands, up along the Burma–Thailand border, through China, along the China–Outer Mongolia border, along the China–Russia border, through Siberia, and out into the Arctic Ocean just north of the Poluostrov Peninsula. All places along this line will experience sunrise simultaneously at 0 hours UT in 2000 or 2001 or any other year. There is simply no unique 'first sunrise' location.

The other interesting dimension is that the time of sunrise is always calculated for sea level. This means that if you go higher, the sunrise is seen earlier. For example, if one was to move 1,000 m above sea level, the sunrise would be visible four minutes and 3.8 seconds earlier than a person at sea level at the same point. Theoretically, this also means that if a person is roughly 100 km west of Katchal but 1,000 m above sea level, he will see this sunrise at about the same time as an observer at Katchal who will be at sea level. The basic argument is that there is nothing spectacularly unique about the sunrise at Katchal. Various permutations and combinations would give the same results.

The arguments over the timing of the new millennium, the time of the sunrise and the exact location could well have been discarded as academic. The logic of raising these points can also be questioned if this unique opportunity had been beneficial to all. But that was precisely the point. There are far greater and serious issues involved in allowing this incorrectly nomenclatured event on the tiny island of Katchal, says Samir Acharya of SANE, who was the first to realize the problems with an event of this nature.

The resident population of Katchal is only 12,000, and nearly 4,000 of these are the Nicobari tribals. The impact of suddenly inducting an additional 20,000 outsiders on this island for a day or two can well be imagined. Acharya points out that this could create a huge health hazard. The presence of 20,000 people means that a minimum of 20,000 to 30,000 kg of human excreta and thousands of litres of liquid waste will be added to the local environment and this will be in addition to unknown quantities of other solid waste like paper and plastic, to name the common ones.

There is another important aspect that was also being ignored. Katchal is the traditional home of the Nicobari tribals. It was designated a tribal reserve under the Andaman and Nicobar Islands Protection of Aboriginal Tribes Regulation (ANPATR) of 1957, and special permissions have to be obtained if outsiders want to visit here.

Additionally, the entire group of Nicobar Islands has always been considered a sensitive area and the entry of foreigners is strictly prohibited. In fact, in the last thirty years, except for one single occasion, not a single tribal pass has been issued to any foreigner to visit the Nicobars. The only exception was the permission given to Rene Dekkar who was specially invited by the Ministry of Environment and Forests (MoEF), Government of India, to study the endangered bird, the megapode, which is found in these islands.

It is significant that in the past, as eminent a person as the legendary Captain Cousteau (of Calypso fame), who wanted to study corals off the Nicobars was denied permission. Renowned institutions like Cambridge University, England, and the Vokkenmuseum (Museum of Anthropology), Berlin, too had their requests to study the wild boar and the famous pottery of Chowra Island turned down. Why then, questioned Acharya, is the island administration taking the retrograde step of permitting 20,000 tourists of unknown vintage to visit Katchal to celebrate the non-event of a pseudo-millennium sunrise? This is the ultimate degenerate step that the government can take, he says.

Besides, there are other fears too. The Andaman and Nicobar Islands are unsurpassed in their botanical wealth, and the ethno-medical knowledge of the tribals who live here is astounding. The possibility cannot be ruled out that the event will become a convenient entry point for bioprospectors and pharmaceutical multinationals who are always on the lookout for newer, virgin areas to explore. Prevention and even a little overcautiousness is certainly a far better option than any corrective action that may be suggested in the future.

A lot of resources and public money are being spent on the event. Recently, a new circuit house in the island, which violates the Coastal Regulation Zone (CRZ), was inaugurated on the island. New work was also being undertaken for the laying of roads and pipelines and the construction of a power-generating station.

For the present, however, the brakes have been applied, though the event itself has not been called off. The decision taken was that the number of tourists will be scaled down from 20,000 to only 2,000. No foreigners will be allowed to land on Katchal or any other island in the Nicobars, but those interested in viewing the sunrise could view it from ships that bring them there. It has also been decided that a Doordarshan crew will be allowed to land on Katchal and record the sunrise for posterity.

The only problem, and surprisingly nobody seems to realize it yet, is that this is the wrong sunrise!

DECEMBER 2004
AND ITS AFTERMATH

Giant clam, Wandoor, South Andaman Island, 1998

A full-grown elephant and a log in the timber yard, Hut Bay, Little Andaman Island, 1998

The Andaman Trunk Road (ATR) at Jirkatang, where it enters the Jarawa Tribal Reserve, 1998

A green sea turtle heads back to the sea after nesting on South Sentinel Island, 1998

Hermit crab, South Sentinel Island, 1998

Jellyfish by the jetty, Ross Island, 1998

At the Uttara Jetty, when the Jarawas came out from the forest for the first time in large numbers, 1998

Two strips of the nest of the edible-nest swiftlet, Baratang Island, 1999

Mangroves, Constance Bay, Jarawa Tribal Reserve, 2002

Breathing roots of a mangrove forest, Mayabundar, Middle Andaman Island, 2003

Fiddler crab amidst the breathing roots of a mangrove forest, Mayabundar, Middle Andaman Island, 2003

Traffic on the ATR as it runs through the heart of the Jarawa Tribal Reserve, 2003

The crab-eating macaque, Great Nicobar Island, 2003

What the Andaman Trunk Road brings to the Jarawas: This is a series of pictures taken on the ATR in February 2003. A passenger bus plying on the ATR slows down as a young Jarawa woman starts to run alongside it.

The woman stretches her hand out as the bus driver passes her something. She transfers it to her right hand and stretches out the other one again.

In this case, it was biscuits that were given to the Jarawa woman. The pictures were submitted to the Supreme Court in 2003 as evidence of the kind of interaction happening on the ATR

This 180° panorama is compilation of eleven photographs taken off the West Coast of Interview Island in February 2005. Huge areas of coral reef in the Andaman Islands have been destroyed in this manner due to uplift caused, primarily, by the tectonic activity of 26 December 2004

The seriously damaged jetty and breakwater, Hut Bay, Little Andaman Island, 2005

The
submerged
forests and
coastline of
Great Nicobar
Island, 2006

Tourists returning from a visit to the
limestone caves, Baratang, 2006

Beach thick-knees, North Cinque Island, 2006

The house crow, one of the many exotics that is establishing itself rapidly in the islands, Baratang Island, 2006

Chestnut-headed bee-eaters, Rutland Island, 2006

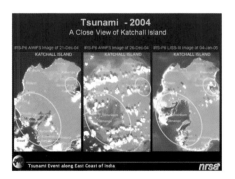

Pre- and post-26 December 2004 satellite images of Katchal and Trinkat islands. Courtesy: NRSA

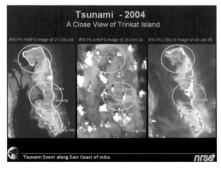

The aftermath of a presidential
visit: stumps of trees chopped
down to facilitate the president's
visit by helicopter, Wandoor,
South Andaman Island, 2008

19

TILT AND TURMOIL IN THE ANDAMANS

Frontline, 25 August 2006

26 DECEMBER 2004 WILL be etched forever in our memories for the tsunami that killed hundreds of thousands of people and caused unprecedented damage in the coastal regions of South and South-East Asia.

Among the worst hit areas in India were the fragile Andaman and Nicobar Islands, particularly the southern group of the Nicobars. Of the nearly 3,500 people reported dead and missing in the entire islands, nearly 3,000 were in the Nicobar group, which has only about 10 per cent of the Andaman and Nicobar Islands' estimated population of 400,000.

Another important indicator of the damage is the area of agricultural and horticultural land that suffered temporary or permanent submergence. In the Nicobars, nearly 6,000 ha (14,826 acres) were damaged, while in the Andamans it was about 1,800 ha (4447.8 acres). The magnitude of the damage to the Nicobars becomes clear when one considers the fact that the Andaman group, with a total area of about 6,400 sq. km, is more than three times the size of the Nicobar group. In the Andamans too much of the damage occurred in the southern parts, in the Little Andaman and South Andaman Islands. The northern groups escaped virtually unscathed.

The explanation for this stark contrast lies in the earthquake that set off the tsunami. The tectonic activity initiated in December 2004 caused a significant shift in the lay of the islands. Assessments done by Roger Bilham of the University of Colorado indicate that the northern parts of the Andaman group of islands experienced a permanent average uplift of 1.2–1.8 m (4–6 ft) while parts of the Nicobars went significantly under – 1.2 m in Car Nicobar and a staggering 4.57 m (15 feet) at the southernmost tip, Indira Point on Great Nicobar Island. The pivot of this swing experienced by the islands can roughly be located south of Port Blair.

In the Nicobars, therefore, the water that the tsunami brought in stayed back, permanently inundating huge areas of coastal and low-lying forest and, where they existed, fields, horticultural plantations and settlements of the Nicobaris and the settler families. Among the most significant but little studied or understood implications of this sudden, phenomenal change in the architecture of the islands is the impact on coastal and marine ecosystems such as mangroves, coastal (littoral) forests and coral reefs. Proof of the damage caused to mangroves and littoral forests lies everywhere in the Nicobars. A continuous wall of submerged, dead, brown, decaying timber of various kinds surrounds every single island. The extensive damage to these forests has also had catastrophic implications for a diverse range of rare and endemic flora and fauna that inhabited these systems.

The submergence in the Nicobars has, for instance, permanently destroyed a major part of the nesting habitat of the Nicobari megapode, an endemic bird that scrapes together a mound of earth for its unique nest. A survey carried out by Ravi Sankaran of the Coimbatore-based SACON in the first few months following the disaster reported that nearly 1,100 nesting mounds were lost in the immediate aftermath of the earthquake and the tsunami.

A survey in early 2006 by K. Sivakumar, who was Sankaran's student and is now with the Wildlife Institute of India in Dehradun, covered nearly 110 km of the coastline in fifteen islands in the Nicobar group. The Nicobari megapode was the subject of his doctoral thesis and he had conducted extensive surveys of the bird during 1993–94. Sivakumar's estimates indicate that there are now only about 500 active nesting mounds of the bird and that its population is less than 30 per cent of what was reported a decade ago. While the bird has been hit badly, fears of its extinction have been put to rest.

Little, unfortunately, is known of the other littoral forest-dwelling fauna, mainly the giant robber crab, the reticulated python and the Malayan box turtle. South Sentinel, a 1.6 sq. km flat, uninhabited island that is also a wildlife sanctuary, had one of the most significant populations of the giant robber crab. Beaching a boat here was always a tricky affair, and after the changes in December 2004, it is reported to have become even more so. No credible scientific information exists of the present situation on this island, and therefore of the crab.

Another ecological system that has been affected on either side of the pivot is the pristine and extensive coral reefs that the islands are famous for. In the Nicobars, the damage was caused by submergence, increased turbidity of water and the sheer physical impact of debris.

Surveys by the Zoological Survey of India (ZSI) have reported significant impact on the coral reefs around the central Nicobar group of islands, including Camorta, Nancowry, Trinket and Katchal. R. Jeyabaskaran of the ZSI's regional station in Port Blair had conducted extensive surveys in the waters of Great Nicobar in 1999. He relooked at the reefs after the tsunami only to find that large coral areas were under debris, sand and mud. He also reported a noticeable reduction in associated coral fauna such as nudibranchs, flat worms, alpheid shrimps and hermit crabs. Another interesting associated change has been the sudden increase in the otherwise uncommon milkfish, *Chanos chanos,* in the Great Nicobar waters. Fisherfolk are now catching them in such large numbers that these have begun to be called the tsunami macchi here.

While the Nicobar coral reefs suffered on account of submergence, those in the Andaman waters were permanently thrust above the high tide line, destroying them almost instantly. Among the first to survey these areas for the changes was Harry Andrews of the Andaman and Nicobar Islands Environment Team. His report and that of Ravi Sankaran for the Nicobars was published as part of a series by the Wildlife Trust of India titled *Ground Beneath the Waves: Post-tsunami Impact Assessment of Wildlife and their Habitats in India'.*

Andrews has estimated that more than 50 sq. km of pristine coral reefs were thoroughly exposed and destroyed, and the largest single area, along the western and northern coast of Interview Island measured 25 sq. km. Like the coral reefs, these parts of the Andamans have also seen loss of mangroves because they are now permanently above the high water mark.

Significantly, most of the experts and others working on ecological issues in the islands have unanimously advocated no intervention as the best form of intervention. 'Allowing nature to take its course is the best way', says Sankaran, 'to allow habitats to restore themselves, and species to colonize areas. Leaving areas alone should be the preferred management option.'

Natural systems are bound to respond in complex ways in an attempt to move towards some kind of equilibrium and this should be allowed to happen. The example of sea turtles is a good one. The beaches of the islands (particularly in the Nicobars) that have been important nesting sites for four species – the giant leatherback, the green sea turtle, the olive ridley and the hawksbill – were all lost when the coastline in the southern group submerged.

In a few months, however, new beaches started to appear, like soothing, soft caresses all along the altered alignments of the ravaged islands. The turtles too were back and there are now regular reports of their using these new beaches for nesting. In the Andamans too many of these exposed reef areas rapidly filled up with sand, creating additional new land masses and new beaches. The process goes on and change continues to happen. What will be the nature of the equilibrium ultimately attained? To obtain the answer, we have to wait and watch.

20

PICKING UP THE THREADS

Frontline, 21 October 2005

A COUPLE OF FISHING boats are gently bobbing up and down in the calm, blue waters of the ocean that is bound on one end by the eastern horizon. Tying it up on the other side is a long strip of sparkling but lonely beach peopled by a few fishermen mending their nets. Eight months after the tsunami's giant landfall in Little Andaman, one is struck by the exceptionally idyllic, albeit extremely deceptive, picture.

This is Hut Bay, the administrative headquarters of Little Andaman Island, 120 km south of Port Blair. Located about halfway between the main group of the Andaman Islands and the southern Nicobar group, Little Andaman is rather inappropriately named. Spread over nearly 730 sq. km, it is not 'little' by any measure; it is, in fact, one of the largest islands in the Andaman and Nicobar group.

The magnitude of the destruction wrought by the waves of 26 December 2004, is palpable at Hut Bay. The jetty was almost entirely damaged as was the small fishing hamlet of Machi Dera, which was, until the tsunami came, a bustling settlement of a couple of hundred families, the first of whom had migrated here in the 1970s from the Srikakulam coast in Andhra Pradesh. Small rectangular plinths are all that remain of the houses. Walls with doors and window frames that stood on these plinths lie scattered; an RCC (reinforced cement concrete) framework, uprooted from its base further away, lies embedded in the sand at an odd angle; a wall that withstood the tidal attack stands, still sporting the name T. VALLABHARAO in bold letters; and on the adjoining plinth stands a rotting wooden column and board with the name G. APPALAMMA across it, like the cross on a tombstone.

There has obviously been post-tsunami activity here, in the hope that it will help and ensure damage assessment and compensation when it finally comes. Joga Rao, who, along with a handful of men, sits mending his nets, points to a small coconut grove about 100 metres away. Five waves hit the coast that morning, he says. The biggest and the most damaging of these, rising to about 9 metres (30 ft), was the fourth one. It topped the coconut trees, according to him, and pushed the water inland for more than a kilometre. In fact, a report submitted in April to the Department of Science and Technology by a team of experts noted that the inland travel of sea water in Little Andaman was more than what was noticed in the Nicobar Islands.

'After the first wave came, it sucked the ocean dry as it went back, exposing the shallow bed of the bay in front of us,' Joga Rao continues. 'People could see hundreds of big and small fish thrashing on the bare bed. Some of them even ran in to pick them up.' But when the wave came back, the residents realized something was wrong and ran inland. Nine people, eight of them women, died in Machi Dera. Had the first wave been a bigger and more powerful one, the casualties and damage would have been much higher.

The entire settlement of Machi Dera was flattened. The community that is dependent on fishing for its livelihood lost almost its entire fleet of 120 boats; all except two were washed away. Both the administration and NGOs have promised to provide new boats, but these are yet to come. Official figures of fish landings here tell the tale of destruction quite clearly. The fish catch in March 2004 was nearly 90,000 kg. In March 2005, it was only about 1,000 kg.

Serious damage was also caused to infrastructure in Hut Bay. The powerhouse located near the beach was inundated and the township had to go without power for many days. The post office, the telephone exchange, the primary health centre and the local branch of the State Bank of India (SBI) also suffered serious damage.

Adjacent to the wall of the SBI complex is a narrow concrete path that leads to the intermediate shelters of Padauk Tikri, home to a few hundred uprooted families. An estimated 6,000 of Little Andaman's 17,000-odd people are currently said to be in one of the five such shelters. Padauk Tikri is now home to the former residents of Machi Dera, where shelters made of plain and corrugated galvanized iron (CGI), have come in for considerable criticism. According to government figures, a total of 1,448 tonnes of these sheets have been used for the construction of nearly 2,000 intermediate shelters in Little Andaman.

At Padauk Tikri, the shelters have been built on a small hillock with a gentle slope. In the initial days, those living

on the top had to haul up water that was supplied by
tankers. Those at the lower end complain about sewage
seeping down from the hillock and entering their shelters.
Work has begun for the construction of a water tank and
the laying of sewerage lines to deal with the problem. It is
clearly a difficult situation. Providing relief and putting up
the intermediate shelters in good time in the face of serious
logistical constraints would have certainly been a difficult
task for the planners and the implementing agencies. The
only concern is whether it could not have been done better.

The same concern is voiced in the intermediate shelters
of Harmander Bay, the Nicobari settlement located a few
kilometres south of Hut Bay. The Nicobarese of Harmander
Bay were brought here from Car Nicobar, the island
immediately south of Little Andaman. Some 160-odd families
were settled here in the 1970s. Their population has grown
and the number of affected families now in the intermediate
shelter is about 400. The drive to this settlement is through
a long stretch of coconut plantations, the most significant
source of livelihood for the Nicobari community. Copra
preparation and trading are their key economic activity. One
of the biggest losses to these islands came from the large-
scale inundation and destruction of the coconut plantations.
The Nicobarese of Harmander Bay are lucky in that their
plantations have survived although the entire settlement
and fifty-odd traditional fishing canoes were washed away.

The waves did spare a small part of their church, the part
with the cross on it. It is a small room with a mezzanine
floor, which was probably at one end of the church. Lying
strewn on the ground are a couple of cane frameworks of
the Christmas star. From a window at the top one can still

see the pulpit at the far end, now completely exposed to the elements. Even the microphone stand is in place, as is the book of hymns from which hymns were probably being sung on that Sunday morning. 'O Lord', begins the first line. The words that follow are not clear as the paper has crumbled.

In the intermediate shelter located behind the coconut plantations, Zita Rachel and Simon run the temporary school for the Nicobari children with the support of Action Aid. Zita also says that of the five waves that hit them, the fourth was the biggest and the most destructive. 'If the first wave had been the size of the fourth,' she says, 'none of us would have survived.' There was no food available for the first few days. While there were coconuts there were no implements to cut them open. The availability of drinking water too was a serious problem, as water sources were damaged by the intrusion of saline water. Initially, there was only one well with potable water, and there was a constant scramble for it. Now, things have slightly improved with tankers supplying water to the shelter.

There is a lot of reconstruction activity going on here. There is the framework for a school building being fabricated in one corner. Some distance away, youth are working hard on the wooden framework of what looks more like a traditional Nicobari dwelling built on stilts. Adjusting to the tin boxes, which have been provided as intermediate shelters, has been difficult for this indigenous community.

Ever since the tragedy struck, the people have been demanding a set of tools that would allow them to begin reconstruction work. But this simple demand was not heeded, not only by the authorities in Harmander Bay, but also those in the rest of the Nicobar Islands.

At Padauk Tikri, the resilient residents did not want to miss out on Ganesh Chaturthi celebrations. A group of young men were seen working frenetically on the construction of a pandal for the festival. Later, in the evening, when we were on board MV *Dering* on our way back to Port Blair, the same bunch of youth were with us. They were on their way to get an idol of Ganesha and the sound system for the festivities that were to start on 7 September.

In more ways than one, this is just the beginning of a long haul for these unfortunate thousands. Many are still scared to go back to the sea or have no boats to resume their occupation. The intermediate shelters are likely to be their home at least for another year and a half, if not more. Also, there is no clarity about where they will be resettled. The local administration and the government are still working out a plan for the re-establishment of the devastated settlements.

As we walked around the shelters, V. Kamesh Rao approached us. 'Will you take a photo?' he asked, pointing to the camera. Soon, he gathered a bunch of children, his own included, and posed for the picture. Also waiting to be photographed was a woman with an empty fish basket on her head. We had seen her earlier in the day, hawking her wares in other parts of the town. It was probably a day of good business. 'My name is S. Barvati,' she said as she put down her basket. And there was a group of enthusiastic children enjoying themselves in the play area who wanted their picture to be taken. Life, indeed, has not lost its charm for these islanders.

21

IGNITED MINDS ON WINGS OF DESIRE

Tehelka, 25 June 2005

PRESIDENT A.P.J. ABDUL KALAM'S penchant for announcing grandiose plans as solutions to problems continue unabated. While the best-known one is his continued advocacy of the monstrous interlinking of India's rivers, the latest victim of his visions could well be the fragile islands of the Andaman and Nicobar, which he visited in May 2005 following the devastating tsunami of 26 December 2004.

He did the normal rounds of places around the islands, particularly in the Nicobar group that has been the worst hit. He visited Car Nicobar, Campbell Bay in Great Nicobar and Teresa in the central Nicobars, and also met representatives of the Nicobari and Shompen tribal communities.

It was on 6 May 2005, at Car Nicobar, while interacting with members of the local community that the president laid out his four-point mission for the development of the islands – deep sea fishing, exploitation of bamboo, value-added coconut products and tourism. The *Daily Telegrams*, the administration's newspaper published from Port Blair, reported the president as saying, 'It [the islands] will be an abode having all the infrastructure to receive and service at least 1 million tourists every year.' He was further reported as saying that Andaman and Nicobar had great potential to be developed on the model of Maldives, where the government leases out entire islands that are then developed by private enterprises as self-contained resorts where the government needs to make no investment.

The proposal has made environmentalists and those working for the rights of the indigenous peoples extremely worried. 'The basis of this projection is not clear,' says Samir Acharya of SANE. 'It is dangerous that the president should suggest something on these lines when it has been proven time and again that the islands do not have the carrying capacity to support more such human activity.'

The total official pre-tsunami population of the islands was a little less than 400,000. Even in that situation, the people of the islands were facing a serious infrastructure problem, including serious water shortages. For many summers now, citizens in large parts of Port Blair have been receiving piped water only once in three days. The problem became so severe that on occasion, water had to be shipped to Port Blair from other islands.

Significantly, the main tourism season here lasts for only about six months, from October to March. The water problem becomes progressively worse as the tourist season progresses and improves only with the setting in of monsoons in mid-May. If this is the situation in Port Blair that has a population of little over 100,000, one can only imagine what will happen when a million people will descend here. What is even more worrying is that in many areas, particularly in the Nicobars, fresh water sources were among the worst hit by the tsunami. While the local community is just about managing to meet its own meagre demands, it is not clear how a million people will be catered to.

There is a crisis here. The islands are presently dealing with basic issues like water, food, infrastructure and housing. Would it not be better (and more ethical) to ensure that rehabilitation and reconstruction are done first in the best and fastest manner possible? Would it not be more sensible, for instance, to assess, first, the bamboo resources of the islands or the coconut plantations? Where are the studies that suggest that these could become the mainstay of the economy?

Very significantly, this island chain is a fragile biodiversity hot spot that is home to a number of extremely vulnerable and threatened indigenous communities like the Jarawa and Onge (in the Andamans) and the Shompen (in the Nicobars). The entire Nicobar group of islands and nearly 20 per cent of the Andamans have been declared a tribal reserve to protect these indigenous people. Already, these communities are significantly outnumbered and marginalized. Suggesting that one million people should be allowed here is an open invitation for disaster.

'This vision demands a concerted response,' says Madhusree Mukerjee, author of *The Land of Naked People*, a hard-hitting historical account of the indigenous people. 'How can someone so educated be so uninformed?' she asks.

'Obviously, the people who matter', she continues, 'are not listening to concerns about carrying capacity, water, coral destruction and other matters that make such a grandiose tourism plan ridiculous in practice.'

Can someone please tell this to the president?

22

SUBSIDIZED TOURISM WORSENS ANDAMAN'S WOES

Inter Press Service, 5 December 2007

TOURISM, PROMOTED AS A major economic activity and employment generator in India's far-flung Andaman Islands, is running into serious opposition. Concerns are being raised, ironically, by local residents and tour operators who are supposed to be the prime beneficiaries.

Increasing awareness of the need to protect forests, dwindling agricultural returns and a continued growth in the population, that now stands at 356,000, has led the government to promote tourism as one of the key areas for economic growth and employment on the islands. Government figures clearly indicate the trend. An estimated 100,000 visitors came to the islands in 2004. The figure was roughly the same for the year 2006 and is expected to cross 150,000 for 2007. While this might not seem like a big jump, the significance becomes obvious when one factors in the tourist numbers for the year 2005. Fewer than 50,000 visited in 2005, in the immediate aftermath of the December 2004 earthquake and the tsunami that followed.

The damage to infrastructure and, more importantly, the uncertainty that followed, hit the islands' fledgling tourism industry hard. Tourist arrivals dropped dramatically, prompting the launch of 'Vitamin Sea', a tourism promotion campaign for the islands. In a related move, the Central government also extended its Leave Travel Concession (LTC) programme to a section of its employees, allowing them free air travel if they chose to holiday in the islands. For nearly two years now, employees from the government-owned Steel Authority of India's units in Bhilai, Bokaro, Durgapur and Rourkela have constituted the bulk of the tourists visiting the islands.

While this might sound like a welcome trend, the fact that a large chunk of these visitors are low-spending domestic tourists is a matter of some consternation. Increasingly, people in Port Blair are complaining that the government policy of promoting tourism, using its own employees, does little good to these tsunami-affected islands.

Such is the resentment against the policy that World Tourism Day, 27 September, saw local tour operators and agencies come out on the streets of Port Blair in protest. Members of the Andaman Chamber of Commerce and Industries point out that the LTC tourists visiting the islands not only spend little money but, through bulk bookings offered by travel agents, use up the scarce resources and facilities and crowd out genuine upmarket tourists.

In a recent article published in a local newspaper, green

campaigner Samir Acharya of SANE wrote: 'Tourism, instead of bringing a boon to the islands, has actually brought a curse on the islanders ... the only contribution [of LTC tourists] to the islands is bringing scarcity of water, [cheap] inter-island boat tickets, island–mainland ship tickets and even air tickets for the localities. What makes it worse and intolerable is that it is totally state-funded.'

The LTC tourists have sorely strained the resources on the islands. The summer of 2007 saw unprecedented water cuts for residents, with parts of Port Blair receiving water only once in five days, and that too for only a couple of hours. 'Due to curtailment of water supply by municipal council,' said a notice put up in the state-run Hotel Megapode in Port Blair at the height of the monsoon season in September, 'all guests are requested not to waste water and not to wash clothes. Water supply timing: Morning 6 a.m. to 10 a.m. Evening 6 p.m. to 10 p.m.' Other restaurants and hotels too have put up notices requesting guests to use water judiciously.

'LTC tourists,' says Zubair Ahmed, a journalist working with the local weekly the *Light of Andamans*, 'are always welcome, if they know in advance what to expect in the islands. LTC tourism is helping the unorganized sector to earn something, but the organized sector is up in arms against it because they are losing their clientele.' Sanjay Ray, a resort owner and an elected representative on Havelock Island, agrees. 'No benefit comes to us from the Indian tourist, and 80 per cent of our benefit comes from foreigners.'

Not everyone, however, disagrees with government policy. New Delhi–based tourism expert and researcher Nina Rao told Inter Press Service (IPS): 'I am surprised at this campaign (World Tourism Day protests). We have always felt that everyone has a right to be a tourist, and this is a democratic right.' However, she adds that tourism should stay within carrying capacity limits. Today, it is established that more than 800 million tourists (around the world) are a serious cause of global warming and this affects island people the most.

While more domestic tourists are being solicited to the islands, little attention has been paid to basic details such as infrastructure, waste management or the impact on sensitive ecosystems like coral reefs. Officials admit privately that the move to boost tourism via the LTC route in the aftermath of the tsunami is backfiring. Evidence of this lies in the fact that the administration recently refused permission to the Indian Railways (the world's largest employer with 1.6 million workers on its rolls) to include the islands as part of its LTC schemes.

Other tourism promotion moves – like the 2005 agreement to twin Port Blair with Thailand's Phuket, 500 km away – have been abandoned following protests by academics and activists that this could have negative social and environmental impacts in the Andamans.

For now, what is certain is that domestic tourism in the Andamans appears to have become a classic case of a remedy being worse than the problem.

23

A VISIT AND AN AFTERMATH

The Hindu, 13 January 2008

WHEN PRESIDENT PRATIBHA PATIL decided to visit the Andaman and Nicobar Islands on the third anniversary of the tsunami in December 2007, it could only have been considered an extremely welcome gesture. For the people of a place ravaged by one of the biggest disasters in living memory, the interest and concern of the first citizen of the country could have been and certainly was a very important statement. Her handing over of 200 permanent houses to citizens in Car Nicobar on 26 December could have and should have made front page news for all the right reasons.

For all the potential and the could-haves, that is not how it turned out in the end. The president's visit to the islands did make front page news, but it was for all the wrong reasons with the responsibility lying mainly at the door of the local administration.

The one issue that perhaps got the maximum attention

was the large-scale tree-cutting seen to coincide with the president's visit. Some media reports indicated that nearly 400 trees had been chopped down across the islands for the visit. While this was not finally and fully confirmed, the administration found itself in a tight corner on account of what happened at Wandoor, near Port Blair. At least sixty full-grown trees that included casuarinas and other local species were chopped down in just this one place to facilitate the president's visit here by helicopter. Wandoor is one of the most visited tourist spots around Port Blair and, as a result, there was significant photographic evidence of what had happened there. A huge amount of money was also spent for increasing the size of the helipad there, for the construction of a special VVIP room and the widening and relaying of the road in the vicinity.

Other decisions taken by the local administration affected local people and the tourism industry in different but equally unreasonable and hard-hitting ways. All advanced bookings for Christmas and New Year's Eve in the administration-run Dolphin Resort on Havelock Island, for instance, were arbitrarily cancelled. Similar cancellations were forced in a number of other government-run places. Shipping services were disrupted, preventing tourists from accessing islands where they had planned a holiday many months earlier and local fishermen were prohibited from going fishing in areas that the president was supposed to visit (Box 12).

There were also concerns over the huge expenses incurred on account of relaying a number of roads and refurbishing guest houses for the visit. The speed at which some of the works were executed has also given rise to fears regarding their quality and durability.

Govind Raju, editor of the local weekly, *The Light of Andamans*, captured the mood and the reaction in his 31 December story titled 'President's 3-day Avalanche'. 'President Pratibha Patil's 3-day excursion in the South Andaman Islands,' he pointed out, 'left a trail of misery for the people of Port Blair and adjacent areas. They were put to all kinds of harassments and discomfiture in the name of security of the first citizen of the country.'

That the focus had been sustained and the issues raised were serious is obvious from the fact that the administration came out with an immediate clarification that these actions had to be taken for security purposes. Their initial explanation, that only pruning was done and that only a few trees had been cut, stood immediately exposed. The local Department of Environment and Forests also pointed out that the cutting of the trees would not create an environmental problem as the casuarinas were planted only to beautify the beach and that, in fact, the felling did not attract the provisions of the Forest Conservation Act.

Conservationists who have been working in the islands, however, point out that a large part of the beach at Wandoor has been destroyed in the last couple of decades on account of sand mining to feed the construction boom of Port Blair. Old uprooted trees that still dot the shoreline here are a grim reminder of that past. They further argue that the felled trees, even if they were a plantation of casuarinas, played an important role as a wind break and also as a protection for the coastal land.

The developments appeared to have even taken Rashtrapati Bhavan by surprise. In statements issued even as the president was still in the islands, it was clarified that neither the president nor her family was spending the new year in the islands and that Rashtrapati Bhavan had not sought cancellation of any room bookings of tourists in view of the president's visit. A clarification has also been sought from the local administration regarding the felling of trees, and instructions have been reportedly issued to undertake compensatory afforestation for the damage caused.

In a move that was clearly aimed at damage control, a symbolic tree plantation by the president was also organized. Photographs released by the Press Information Bureau (PIB) showed her planting a casuarina sapling at the very site where the sixty trees had been cut at Wandoor. While this too can be considered a welcome gesture, it was clearly the classic case of too little, too late.

A researcher following the developments related to the president's visit to the islands had this to say, following reports of the symbolic tree plantation: 'I visited Wandoor immediately after the president's visit, but could not find the sapling she planted anywhere.'

Maybe he was looking in the wrong place or maybe it was just a tongue-in-cheek comment. Either way, the irony and the contradictions cannot be missed.

Box 12: In the name of the President

- Havelock off limit for tourists on 26 and 27 December.
- Fishermen of Wandoor, Guptapara and Port Blair not to venture out into the sea on 28 December.
- Wandoor out of bounds on 28 December.
- Fishermen of Neil and Havelock Islands prohibited from fishing on 27 December.
- Sound and Light Show closed for tourists on 25 and 26 December.
- National Memorial Cellular Jail closed for visitors on 26 December.
- Private Harbour Cruise not to berth at Aberdeen Jetty on 26 December.
- All the sailings to Havelock and Neil Island cancelled on 27 December.
- Directorate of Shipping Services office closed on 27 December.
- Restricted holiday on 24 December cancelled.
- Hotel bookings in Hornbill Nest and Dolphin Resort cancelled and advance returned.

Source: *The Light of Andamans*, Port Blair, 31 December 2007.

ACADEMIC PAPERS

24

DISASTER AS A CATALYST FOR MILITARY EXPANSIONISM – THE CASE OF THE NICOBAR ISLANDS

Economic and Political Weekly, 3 January 2015[1]

BrahMos Strikes in the Andamans

IT WAS EARLY MARCH 2008, when, on a train journey from Pune to Jodhpur, I received a series of phone calls from television and print journalists seeking my opinion about an event that had occurred earlier that day in the Andaman Islands. The first call was from the environment

[1] The paper was first presented at the 'Manifestations of History in the Andaman Islands' conference held in June 2013 at the Institute for Ethnologie, Munich University, Germany. I would like to thank Frank Heidemann, Philipp Zehmisch, Manish Chandi, Ramanujam Venkat and Nimesh Ved for their comments and inputs.

correspondent of the CNN-IBN news channel. She wanted
to know what I thought would be the environmental
consequences of the successful testing of the BrahMos missile
that had reportedly hit a target on an Andaman Island only
a few hours ago. I was completely unprepared for this. Not
only had I not known anything of this test (no one knew
about it), I knew nothing about the BrahMos missile itself.

I explained to her, as also to the string of subsequent
callers, that I knew nothing of this test and nothing at all
could be said of its impact unless some more information
was available on what had happened. One particular detail
was immediately of great interest to me – the island in the
Andaman group that was the target of this missile test. I put
this question to all those who called because (a) I wanted
to know myself, and (b) unless this was known, speaking
of environmental consequences would be meaningless.
Surprisingly, not one of the many people who wanted my
opinion had an answer to my question. All they knew was
that the BrahMos missile had hit an island in the Andaman
group and had done so with pinpoint accuracy.

I was as struck by the fact that they did not know the
exact location as by their insistence that it was an Andaman
Island. This was, in any case, the story they had officially
received. Prima facie, it seemed unlikely to me that it could
have been the Andamans. For one, the Andaman group of
islands are reasonably well inhabited, particularly the larger
land mass that comprises the islands of South Andaman,
Middle Andaman, North Andaman and Baratang. There are
a number of outlying islands, but it was difficult to agree
immediately that any of these could have been the target of
this missile. These were too close to the inhabited parts of the

island system and the risk of a test gone wrong seemed too big for the establishment to take. Additionally, a number of these uninhabited outlying islands in the Andaman group have been declared as wildlife sanctuaries under the provisions of the Wild Life Protection Act, 1972. Though the defence and security imperative often allows for environmental and wildlife protection concerns to be ignored, it seemed unlikely to me that it could have happened in this case without at least some information of it being available in the public domain. It was more likely, it seemed to me even then, that the island that was targeted was in the Nicobar group. There was no way, however, to confirm this and all the journalists who had called were speaking in one voice of an Andaman island.

Was It the Nicobars Then?

This was the story that was carried over the next few days in all media reports; significantly, even in the press release issued by the Press Information Bureau of the Government of India itself:

A naval version of the BrahMos cruise missile was successfully tested *off Andamans coast* this morning. The missile was launched from the decks of INS *Rajput* at 10.30 a.m. and precisely hit a land target in one of the islands of Andaman and Nicobar. Defence Research and Development Organization (DRDO) scientists said the missile met all flight parameters during its launch, flight, and zeroed in on the designated target among the group of targets, destroying it with a thunderous blast (PIB 2008).

The only exception to this was *The Hindu,* which noted that the BrahMos missile 'destroyed a target on an uninhabited island in the Nicobar group of islands situated in the Andaman and Nicobar archipelago' (Anon. 2008). This was the first indication to me that my suspicion about the target being a Nicobar island may have been right, but there was still no way to confirm this. There was absolutely no further information in the public domain and over the next few days I contacted a number of people who either live in the islands or closely follow developments there to answer this puzzle. This included journalists based both in New Delhi and Port Blair, researchers who have travelled extensively in the islands and others with access to the corridors of power. None was able to provide an answer.

It was only many months later that the conundrum in my head found a resolution. This information is still not available in the public domain, but there is reason to believe we now know what happened on that day in the first half of March 2008. We were able to confirm through sources in the establishment and also in the islands that the target was indeed in the Nicobars – the little island of Trak, located in the southern group of the Nicobars – an island so small that most maps do not show it and even if they do, more often than not, it remains unidentified.

It could well be that the establishment was being less than rigorous in talking of the Andaman Islands; the identity of the Nicobar group of islands has always been subsumed by that of its larger neighbour to the north. The non-naming of the particular island also has an explanation, perhaps, in the realms of important strategic and military thinking, but

I have always wondered (and continue to wonder) what this imperative could be.

This successful testing, though quite remarkable from many angles, would have been something to note and then be forgotten; there are, after all, any number of defence-related manoeuvres, testing and pronouncements that we read and hear of regularly from different parts of the country. As I have continued to follow the developments in these islands over the years, however, I realized that the BrahMos test was not an isolated event. There have, in fact, been a string of significant defence-related happenings, particularly in the Nicobar Islands, in the last few years. And it is this series of events that lies at the heart of the hypothesis I intend to present here.

January 2009: Meroe and Passage Islands

In January 2009, only a few months after the successful testing of the BrahMos missile with Trak as a target, we got information from within the A&N administration that the defence establishment was seeking more permissions. This time it was for the island of Meroe, not very far from Trak. The queries were related to the wildlife, forests and the environment of the island – a search was going on for another island to use as a missile launching site or perhaps as a target, as in the case of Trak. The Forest Department of the A&N administration was asked to provide information on the biodiversity value of this island before a decision of some sort could be taken.

Though presently uninhabited, Meroe Island has

traditionally belonged to the islanders of Kondul, Little Nicobar and some of Pilo Milo and they have also had their settlements here in the past. They still have plantations there, and there are a number of legends associated with past human habitation as well as the animals found there. The island is a known breeding colony of the white-tailed, tropical bird *Phaethon lepturus* and is also home to other endangered fauna that includes the robber crab *Birgus latro*, the Nicobari megapode, *Megapodius nicobariensis* and the saltwater crocodile. The small beaches of the island are also used regularly for nesting by the green sea turtle *Chelonia mydas* and hawksbill turtle *Eretmochelys imbricata*.

At about the same time, a local researcher informed me that other islands in the vicinity, Passage Island for instance, were being regularly used by the navy for firing practice and that there had been firing practice on Treis Island as well. The residents of Little Nicobar Island who have plantations on Treis had, in fact, been asked to keep away for a while when the practice was on.

It is quite likely that Passage, Treis and other islands in the region have been regularly used for defence-related activities for a very long time, but the testing of the BrahMos missile and the exploration of Meroe as another site were new developments that point towards the emergence of a new equation.

February 2009: Camorta

Just a month later, in February 2009, a serious disagreement broke out between the navy and the Nicobari community in the Nancowry group of islands. The disagreement was over the ownership on Camorta Island of 128 ha of land owned by the defence (including over 81 ha by the navy), with the local community and the defence establishment accusing each other of encroachment. INS *Kardip*, the naval base, has been there since the early 1980s, and though the matter was eventually resolved in New Delhi (Anon. 2009a), the flaring up of the conflict was clearly an indication of a heightened interest and proposed intensification of military activity in the region.

September 2009: Militaristic Vision for the Islands

Later that year, in September 2009, the Andaman and Nicobar Command (ANC), India's first integrated tri-services command, held a national seminar on 'Security and Development of the Andaman and Nicobar Islands' in Port Blair. The vision for 2020 for the islands as outlined by the chief guest, former president A.P.J. Abdul Kalam, was prominently militaristic. His proposal included among other things the construction of:

> A 250 MW nuclear power station on one of the islands for A&N exclusively, (...) bases for static aircraft carrier with dynamic warfare system and connectivity between the islands with fibre-optic network, a nuclear submarine-based fleet and (...) a robust tsunami forecasting and communication system (Anon. 2009b).

While this vision was not exclusively about the Nicobars (the Andamans too were included), the scale of intervention proposed and its hugely technocratic-militaristic tenor is in line with the growing defence and strategic interest in this group of islands.

November 2011: Tillangchong Island

A couple of years later, in November 2011, there was news that the Indian Navy had put in a proposal for setting up a temporary target for firing practice on the Tillangchong Island (Anon. 2011; Chandi 2012) which is a stronghold of the endemic and threatened Nicobari megapode. This island in the Nancowry group is at once a wildlife sanctuary under the provisions of the Wild Life Protection Act, 1972 (Amended 2006) (Pande et al. 1991), a tribal reserve as notified under the Andaman and Nicobar Protection of Aboriginal Tribes Regulation, as amended in 2004, an internationally recognized important bird area (Zafar-ul-Islam and Rahmani 2004) and also an island that is of great customary and ritual importance for the Nicobari tribal community (Chandi 2012).

It was only in late 2012, after a sustained campaign in the media, particularly by wildlife and environmental NGOs that the Ministry of Environment and Forests of the Government of India issued an order (Khanduri 2012) rejecting the proposal on grounds of the 'high conservation values' of the place. Not only had the wildlife and biodiversity value of the place been given short shrift in the proposal, the laws and regulations related to tribal rights had also been ignored.

August 2012: INS *Baaz*, Great Nicobar Island

At about the time that the Tillangchong proposal was being hotly debated, another significant event occurred further south. INS *Baaz* was commissioned at Campbell Bay on Great Nicobar Island, as the first naval air station in the Nicobar Islands. The air station is presently equipped to operate light to heavy aircraft capable of short field operations from the runway of about 1,067 m (3,500 ft). Future plans include the extension of the runway to enable unrestricted operation of all categories of aircraft, including heavy aircraft, and to introduce modern airfield instruments and navigation aids (Anon. 2012).

The sentiment about the Andaman and Nicobar Islands in the thinking of the Indian defence establishment was revealed in the address on the occasion by Admiral Nirmal Verma, Chief of Naval Staff:

> The islands of the Andaman and Nicobar group have always occupied the consciousness of the security and defence community of our nation. The geographic disposition of the archipelago, separated as it is by more than 650 nautical miles from our mainland, offers a vital geostrategic advantage to India. Not only do they provide the nation with a commanding presence in the Bay of Bengal, the islands also serve as our window into east and south-east Asia. India's Look East policy has certainly benefited due to the proximity of this archipelago to many ASEAN states. Apart from geography, the economic potential of the islands is also remarkable, being endowed with a vast Exclusive Economic Zone, accounting for almost 30 per cent of India's entire

EEZ. They also sit astride some of the busiest shipping lanes of the Indian Ocean, most carrying strategic cargo for the East Asian economies (Verma 2012).

Admiral Verma's address epitomizes the view with which the Andaman and Nicobar Islands have been looked at from the very beginning – as hugely significant strategic and economic nodes. In a fast-changing, international economic and security environment, the islands have become an even more highly valued asset. The defence presence in these islands has also always been a prominent reality and plans and proposals have always been in the air and in various stages of execution.

Military Activities: Not a Coincidence

It is within this larger context of history and of geography that we need to place all the developments in the Nicobars listed above. It is also possible that many of these have actually been in the pipeline for long and have come to fruition only now. But it is remarkable that in a short span of a few years, there has been such an escalation of military interest and activity in the Nicobar Islands. Importantly, this is mainly information that is available in the public domain and it is quite likely that there are other projects and initiatives at various stages of discussion and planning at various points within the establishment. Was there something to this string of developments? Was there a pattern? Is there something to be said for the location of all these activities in the Nicobar Islands?

My primary and, needless to say, tentative contention is that the clustering of these military activities in the Nicobar Islands in this recent period is not just a coincidence. It is suggestive of the emergence of a new equation, the outcome itself of the devastating earthquake and tsunami of December 2004. The evidence is only circumstantial and the conclusions inferential, but here is the proposition or question that I would like to place: Is it likely that the devastation that was brought upon these islands in December 2004, particularly in the Nicobars, helped germinate the idea that the washed-out islands are now even more fertile territory for defence activity? A group of islands, which has always only existed on the margins of the consciousness of the nation, becomes even more legitimate territory in the strategic vision of the state. In any case, as we have seen already, many important echelons of power view these islands primarily as a security and economic adjunct to the nation state. Did the earthquake and tsunami further reify the fringe-ness of the fringe, allowing for experimentation, explosions and targeting in the interests of the Centre?

What land but the most wasted could be used as a target for testing of the BrahMos? Why would Meroe Island be scouted for as another such site if it could have been put to any other use in spite of the fact that it is and always has been used by the local Nicobari communities? Why ask for permission for a firing range on Tillangchong, an island that is known to be rich in biodiversity value and also of cultural importance for the local community? Why has it been forgotten (or was it ignored) that the entire group of Nicobar Islands – Trak, Treis, Meroe and Tillangchong included – is protected as tribal reserve[2] under the law of the land (ANPATR, 1956, as amended in 2004).

It is my contention that the answer, as least part of it, lies in the unprecedented tectonic upheaval of 26 December 2004 and all that occurred in the immediate aftermath. The Nicobars were indeed washed out in a manner that has still not been fully recognized, leave alone understood. It is in the notion of a washed-out land- and waterscape far away from the centres of power in mainland India that lies the genesis of this new and changing equation. It is this that I now turn to, and for this I will rely primarily on previously published work (Sekhsaria 2009) that highlights the details and the sequence of events that occurred on that fateful day.

December 2004

The date, 26 December 2004, is remembered today for the tsunami that struck large parts of South and South-East Asia, killing hundreds of thousands of people and causing destruction that runs into billions of dollars. In the Andaman and Nicobar Islands, particularly the Nicobars, this image of the tsunami as the primary destroyer is an incomplete one. The tsunami had a significant role to play for sure, but importantly, the earthquake that caused the tsunami in the first place also needs to be implicated in the consequences.

The earthquake of 26 December 2004 and the tsunami

---

[2] The only exception is a strip of land along the east coast of Great Nicobar Island that was excluded from tribal reserve status (ANPATR, 1956, as amended in 2004). This strip is the location of Campbell Bay, the administrative headquarters of the island, a few non-tribal settlements and INS *Baaz*.

that came in its wake are the biggest disaster to have hit the islands in living memory (Andrews and Vaughan 2005; Anon. 2006; Malik and Murthy 2005; Sankaran 2005). This is not surprising considering that Indira Point, the southernmost tip of the islands located on Great Nicobar Island (6°45'12"N, 93°49'36"E) is located only about 180 km. from the epicentre of the earthquake that triggered the tsunami. Official figures list 3,513 people as either dead or missing, 7,992 ha[3] as the paddy and plantation land that was affected, 938 boats as being fully damaged, while the number of livestock reported to have been lost in the disaster was 157,577 (Anon. 2006; Chandi undated) (Tables 5 and 6).

Disaggregated figures along the Island Groups

Disaggregation of these figures along the lines of the two island groups – the Andamans and the Nicobars – gives a very interesting and important picture. Of the 3,513 people reported dead and missing, only sixty-four are from the Andaman group of islands, the remaining 3,449 being from various islands in the Nicobar group. Of the total agricultural and paddy land destroyed, 76 per cent is from the Nicobar group. Similarly, 80 per cent of livestock loss was in the Nicobars. Figures of houses being constructed for the tsunami-affected in 2006 also indicate a similar trend. Of the 9,797 permanent houses being constructed, 7,001 or 71 per cent were in the Nicobars (Anon. 2006).

---

[3] A subsequent statistic from the A&N administration indicates that the total agricultural land lost was 10,837 hectares of which 9,107 hectares was said to be plantation land while 1,730 hectares was paddy land. The island-wise break-up for this figure is not available.

It is evident that the impact in the Nicobar group of islands was much worse than that in the Andaman Islands. While the Nicobar Islands account for only 22 per cent and 12 per cent of the area and population, respectively, of the entire chain of islands, 98 per cent of the deaths and 76 per cent of loss of agricultural land occurred here. The damage caused was inversely proportional to the area and population of the two groups and strikingly so (Tables 5 and 6).

The Earthquake

While the tsunami was directly responsible for a large part of the damage, a more fundamental explanation lies in the earthquake that caused the tsunami. While the tectonic movements triggered by the earthquake catalysed the tsunami, they also caused a huge and permanent shift in the lay of the Andaman and Nicobar Islands. Preliminary reports and assessments showed that with a pivot figuratively and roughly located near Port Blair, parts of the Andaman Islands in the north experienced permanent uplift of 1–2 metres while there was a subsidence of up to 4 metres in some parts of the Nicobar group of islands (Bilham et al. 2005; Malik and Murthy 2005; Ramanamurthy et al. 2005; Thakkar and Goyal 2006).

The tide gauge at Port Blair is reported to have recorded initial subsidence of the harbour (or rise in sea level) about thirty-eight minutes after local shaking commenced (Bilham et al. 2005). News reports and eyewitness accounts indicate that the main shocks were felt in Port Blair around 6.30 a.m. and 6.35 a.m. on 26 December 2004. While this was followed almost immediately (fifteen to twenty minutes later) by the

Table 5: Island-wise losses

ISLAND	PEOPLE (DEAD or MISSING)		LIVESTOCK LOSS		AGRICULTURAL LAND LOST		PERMANENT HOUSING		TOTAL AREA		POPULATION (2001)	
	Total Number	%	Total Number	%	Area in Hectares	%	Number	%	Sq. km	%	Number	Per cent
ANDAMANS	64	2	31,521	20	1,877	23.5	2,796	28.6	6,408	77.68	314,048	88.1
South Andaman	7		19,634		1,667		823					
Little Andaman	54		11,165		117		1,973					
Middle Andaman			722		93							
NICOBARS	3,449	98	126,056	80	6,115	76.5	7,001	71.4	1,841	22.32	42,068	11.9
Car Nicobar	854		50,350		969.35		3,941					
Chowra	117		11,896		230.4		346					
Teresa			17,307		743.96		506					
Katchal	1,551		18,678		1,628.5		315					
Nancowry	378		1,440		256.57		269					
Camorta			7,501		637.4		518					
Trinket			2,590		328.5							
Little Nicobar			2,267				111					
Great Nicobar	549		12,298		1,291.28		995					
Kondul			336									
Pilo Milo			823									
Bampoka			570		29.55							
TOTAL	3513	100	157,577	100	7,992	100	9,797	100	8,249	100	356,252	100

Table 6: Losses in percentage, island-wise

	Andaman (%)	Nicobar (%)	Total
Area (sq. km)	6,408 (77.68)	1,841(22.32)	8,249
Population (2001)	314,048 (88)	42,068 (12)	356,252
People (Dead or Missing)	64 (2)	3,449 (98)	3,513
Livestock Loss	31,521 (20)	126,056 (80)	157,577
Agricultural Land Lost (hectares)	1,877 (23.5)	6,115 (76.5)	7,992
Permanent Housing	2,796(28.6)	7,001 (71.4)	9,797

first influx of sea waves, it was around 8.30 a.m., two hours after the main shock, that a third wave is supposed to have hit the shores with a velocity that caught citizens unaware (Anon. 2004a, 2005b).

The Nicobars Are the Worst Hit

Other reports indicate that there was a gap of fifty minutes between the initial earthquake and the first wave of the tsunami in Port Blair. Three more waves are reported to have followed with a gap between each of thirty to thirty-five minutes. While there is no information to indicate what may have happened in other parts of the islands, it can perhaps be assumed that the pattern elsewhere was similar. By implication, the huge subsidence that has been reported in parts of the Nicobars occurred along with or before the intensely damaging waves of the tsunami hit the shores of the islands. The Nicobars, though spread over a smaller area and also more thinly populated, suffered much larger damages than the Andamans and this is precisely what is reflected in the figures of those killed as also of agricultural and horticultural land lost.

The dominant human population in the Nicobar Islands is the Nicobari tribal community that is primarily coast dwelling (Singh 2006). They were in the direct route of the powerful tsunami which followed the significant subsidence that had taken place on account of the earthquake and were, therefore, the most vulnerable. Of the 3,513 people reported dead or missing, 3,449 were in the Nicobars and of these, 2,955 were indeed from the tribal communities of this island group (Anon. 2006).

Ecological Changes in the Nicobars

The significance, magnitude and implications of the tectonic shifts that happened can also be inferred by looking at the ecological changes that were engendered. Significant change was reported almost immediately along the coastline of most of these islands. The small Megapode Island located west of Great Nicobar, for instance, went completely under (Manish Chandi, personal communication). Coral reefs, beaches and low-lying coastal forests across the Nicobars were badly affected. The reefs in the offshore waters too were hit due to a combination of the submergence, the resultant increase in turbidity and the physical damage caused by tonnes of debris thrown back and forth by the furious waves. A survey conducted by the Zoological Survey of India reported large-scale sedimentation on coral reefs around Great Nicobar Island after the tsunami. A reduction in the number of other associated coral reef fauna including nudibranchs, flat worms, alpheidae and mantis shrimps and hermit and brachyuran crabs was also reported (Alfred, Jeyabaskaran and Rao 2006).

In an interesting development immediately after the tsunami, fishermen from Campbell Bay in Great Nicobar reported a sudden and huge increase in the catch of milkfish *Chanos chanos*, which was relatively rare earlier. So huge and sustained was the harvest of this particular fish that it quickly came to be called the 'tsunami macchi' (Anon. 2005a). While the exact causes can only be speculated about, a post-tsunami ocean salinity and temperature study carried out in the islands by scientists of the National Centre for Antarctic and Ocean Research did find considerable thermohaline variability in the upper 300-metre column of ocean water and concluded that changes like this could be expected to have a significant impact on primary production and fisheries (Luis, Pednekar and Sudhakar 2007).

A Changed Coastline

Early surveys conducted by ANET in the Nicobars also indicated huge losses of pandanus (*Pandanus leram*) and the nipa palm (*Nypa fruticans*). The nipa palm in particular was wiped out almost completely from the estuarine regions of Little Nicobar and Great Nicobar Islands. Significantly, both these plants are extremely important for the Nicobari community as a source of food and materials for regular use like thatch for their dwellings (Chandi 2005a, 2005b, 2006, undated).

The permanent submergence in the Nicobars also saw the immediate and complete loss of most of the beaches here, many of which were important nesting sites for the four marine turtle species found here (Chandi et al 2006; Murugan 2006). The damage to the low-lying coastal areas, the coastal forests and the mangroves, however, was a much more permanent one. Large tracts of these forests were completely destroyed and for many months after the disaster, the islands in the Nicobars could be seen encircled by an endless brown wall of dying and decaying trees. A study of the central group of Nicobar Islands (Nancowry, Camorta, Trinket and Katchal), based on remote sensing and geographic information system (GIS), conducted by the Institute for Ocean Management at Chennai's Anna University assessed the range of damages from 51 per cent to 100 per cent for mangrove ecosystems, 41 per cent to 100 per cent for coral reef ecosystems and 6.5 per cent to 27 per cent for forest ecosystems (Ramachandran et al. 2005).

Ravi Sankaran of SACON conducted a rapid impact assessment of the Nicobars almost immediately after the disaster. His main interest was to look at the status of the Nicobari megapode. The submergence in the Nicobars had permanently destroyed a huge part of the birds' nesting habitat and the study found that nearly 1,100 nesting mounds had been lost (Sankaran 2005). A subsequent survey in early 2006 by the Wildlife Institute of India covered nearly 110 km of the coastline in fifteen islands in the Nicobar group. The study estimated that only about 500 active nesting mounds of the bird had survived in the Nicobars and that the megapode population post-tsunami was less than 30 per cent of what had been estimated during surveys conducted nearly a decade ago (Sivakumar 2006). The result was a direct outcome of the loss of habitat on account of permanent submergence. Significantly, the Tillangchong Island, which the navy wanted for firing practice, remains a significant stronghold of this endemic bird.

The changes that have occurred in the islands, their magnitude and sheer physicality are indeed overwhelming. These changes, I am proposing, are the foundation on which subsequent developments and the increased militarization of the islands are premised.

General Perception

What has been presented here as evidence of the magnitude of change was, obviously, not available in the immediate aftermath of the monumental events. The experiences were there, however, as can be seen from how the media reported the islands in the first few weeks after.

The impact on the defence establishment and infrastructure, particularly the very important air force base on Car Nicobar Island, was prominent in the first set of news reports about the islands (Anon. 2004a; Dikshit 2004; Aroor 2005).

Similarly, not surprisingly, and important for the case I seek to make, the defence establishment was asked to and immediately played a key role in relief and rehabilitation in the far-flung, remote and poorly connected islands: 30 December: 'Army Launches "Seawave" (Anon. 2004b); 31 December: 'IAF Starts Island Evacuation' (Anon. 2004c); 1 January: 'Navy, Coast Guard Step Up Assistance' (Radhakrishnan 2005); and 3 January: 'Integrated Defence Staff Directs Relief' (Anon. 2005). The defence establishment did indeed play a key role, providing help and relief that is and will continue to be appreciated by the island's inhabitants. No one else, in any case, was equipped to launch the kind of exercise that was needed even though many have argued it was not enough in the face of the scale of the damage caused and the assistance needed.

The defence establishment witnessed first-hand the scale and the nature of the destruction that happened, the changes this forced on the islands and the people who live there. A number of islands or at least prominent settlements on many islands were completely abandoned in the immediate aftermath. It has taken many years for some semblance of normality to return.

It is my contention that these huge tectonic, spatial and socio-economic changes in the landscape, seaspace and people-scape of the Nicobars have filtered a certain image of the islands through the layers in the defence establishment. I cannot present it as a well-framed picture, because I myself do not know what it is, but its broad contours can clearly be discerned.

Conclusions

The strategic value of these islands has been explicitly articulated by those in power for many decades now and the evidence of a growing presence of the military establishment is too strong to ignore; it is, in fact, overwhelming. It is also evident in the statements like those of the former president quoted above and also in other articulations of analysts like Ashok Malik (2014) when, in a recent article on the strategic importance of these islands, he describes them as a 'prized piece of mid-ocean real estate'. The defence interests and establishment in the islands are like a huge jigsaw of which the earthquake and tsunami are only one piece. The larger question that needs to be looked into is the long-term and larger implication of this for the people, environment and biodiversity of these islands. There are many cases around the world, particularly of islands that have become mere extensions of larger political, economic and strategic interests. The Nicobar Islands appear clearly to be headed in that direction, if they are not already there!

References

Alfred, J.R.B., R. Jeyabaskaran and D.V. Rao (2006), 'Impact of Tsunami on Biodiversity of Andaman and Nicobar Islands', *Envis Newsletter*, 21 April, (1&2), 2–5.

Andrews, H.V. and A. Vaughan (2005), 'Ecological Assessment in the Andaman Islands and Observations in the Nicobar Islands', in R. Kaul and V. Menon (eds), *The Ground Beneath the Waves: Post-tsunami Impact Assessment of Wildlife and their Habitats in India*, Vol. 2, New Delhi: Wildlife Trust of India.

Andaman and Nicobar Protection of Aboriginal Tribes Regulation Including all Amendments till 2004, No. 4 CFR (Code of Federal Regulation), Andaman and Nicobar Administration (2004).

Anon. (2004a), '1000 Dead in Andamans, Air Force Base Washed Off', *The Times of India*, 27 December 2004.

Anon. (2004b), 'Army Launches "Seawave"', *The Times of India*, 30 December 2004.

Anon. (2004c), 'IAF Starts Island Evacuation', *The Asian Age*, 31 December 2004.

Anon. (2005), 'Integrated Defence Staff Directs Relief', *The Asian Age*, 3 January 2005.

Anon. (2005a), 'Potential Tiger Shrimp Ground Reported from C/ Bay', *The Daily Telegrams,* 18 July 2005.

Anon. (2005b), 'A Preliminary Report on Investigation of Effects of the Sumatra-Andaman Earthquake of 26 December 2004 in the

Andaman and Nicobar Islands', New Delhi: Geological Survey of India, 2005.

Anon. (2006), *Andaman and Nicobar Islands: Towards a Brighter Tomorrow*, Port Blair: A&N Administration.

Anon. (2008), 'BrahMos Test-fired', *The Hindu,* 6 February 2008.

Anon. (2009a), 'ANC Clarifies Its Stand', *The Daily Telegrams,* 14 February 2009.

Anon. (2009b), 'Kalam Inaugurates Seminar on Security and Development of Andaman and Nicobar', http://andamanchronicle.com/content/view/1464/27/ (accessed on 13 February 2013).

Anon. (2011), 'Navy's Andaman & Nicobar Missile Test Plan Hits Green Hurdle', *The Times of India,* 9 November 2011.

Anon. (2012), 'INS Baaz Commissioned as First Naval Air Station in Nicobar Islands', 2012, http://www.indiandefencereview.com/news/ins-baaz-commissioned-as-first-naval-air-station-in-nicobar-islands/ (accessed on 13 February 2013).

Aroor, S. (2005), 'The Air Force Station That Just Vanished', *The Indian Express,* 1 January 2005.

Bilham, R., E.R. Engdahl, B. Feldl and S.P. Satlyalbala (2005), 'Partial and Complete Rupture of the Indo-Andaman Plate Boundary 1847-2004', *Seism Res Lett,* 76(3), 299–311.

Chandi, M. (2005a), *A Note on the Rehabilitation Requirements of the Islands of Little Nicobar, Pulomilow and Kondul of the Southern Nicobar Islands*, Port Blair: Reefwatch Marine Conservation and Andaman and Nicobar Environment Team, 2005.

—— (2005b), *Report of a Visit and Survey (1) of Little Nicobar and Great Nicobar Islands from March 13 to 22*, Port Blair: Reefwatch Marine Conservation and Andaman and Nicobar Environment Team.

—— (2006), *Participatory Regeneration of Nypa Fruiticans: A Resource Augmentation Program in the Southern Nicobar Islands*, Port Blair: Andaman and Nicobar Environment Team, Madras Crocodile Bank Trust.

—— (2012), 'Targetting Tillangchong', *The Hindu Sunday Magazine,* 22 January 2012.

—— (undated), *Name of Tuhet Plantation Places on Pulomilo Island, A Short Report,* Port Blair: Andaman and Nicobar Environment Team.

Chandi, M., S. Paung, S. Agu, S. Poricha, S. John and A. Vaughan (2006), 'Notes and Observations on Flora and Fauna during a Survey of the Coastline and Sea Turtle Nesting Beaches of the Andaman Islands: A Report to the Andaman and Nicobar Environment Team', Port Blair: Andaman and Nicobar Environment Team, 22 January 2006, p. 39.

Dikshit, S. (2004), 'Plan to Station Sukhoi-30 Fighters in Andamans Put on Hold', *The Hindu,* 29 December 2004.

Khanduri, S.K. (2012), 'Office Memorandum: Permission for Erection of Structure Within Tillangchong Sanctuary, Andaman and Nicobar Islands for Temporary Use by Indian Navy' – reg (F No 6-18/ 2011/WL-I), New Delhi: Government of India.

Luis, A.J., S.M. Pednekar and M. Sudhakar (2007), 'Post-tsunami Impact Study on Thermohaline Structure in the Bay of Bengal', *Current Science,* 93(5), 699–703.

Malik, A. (2014), 'Our String of Islands Theory', *Hindustan Times,* 1 September 2014.

Malik, A.J., and C.V.R. Murthy (2005), 'Landscape Changes in Andaman and Nicobar Islands (India) Due to Mw 9.3 Tsunamigenic Sumatra Earthquake of 26 December', *Current Science,* 88(9), 1384–86.

Murugan, A. (2006), 'The Effect of Tsunami on Sea Turtle Nesting Beaches along the Coast of India', paper presented at the Second International Symposium on SEASTAR2000 and Asian Bio-logging Science, Bangkok, December 2005.

Pande, P., A. Kothari and S. Singh, (eds.) (1991), *Directory of National Parks and Sanctuaries in Andaman and Nicobar Islands: Management Status and Profiles,* New Delhi: Indian Institute of Public Administration.

Press Information Bureau (2008), 'BrahMos Naval Version

Tested Successfully', 2008. http://pib.nic.in/newsite/erelease. aspx?relid=36060 (accessed on 13 February 2013).

Radhakrishnan, R.K. (2005), 'Navy, Coast Guard Step Up Assistance', *The Hindu,* 1 January 2005.

Ramachandran S., S. Anitha, V. Balamurugan, K. Dharanirajan, K.E. Vendhan, M.I.P. Divien and A. Udayaraj (2005), 'Ecological Impact of Tsunami on Nicobar Islands' (Camorta, Katchal, Nancowry and Trinket), *Current Science,* 2005, 89(1), 195–200.

Ramanamurthy, M.V., S. Sundaramoorthy, Y. Pari, V.R. Rao, P. Mishra, M. Bhat and B.R. Subramanian (2005), Innundation of sea water in Andaman and Nicobar Islands and Parts of the Tamil Nadu Coast during 2004 Sumatra Tsunami', *Current Science,* 88(11), 1736–40.

Sankaran, R. (2005), 'Impact of the Earthquake and the Tsunami on the Nicobar Islands', in R. Kaul and V. Menon (eds.), *The Ground Beneath the Waves: Post-Tsunami Impact Assessment of Wildlife and Their Habitats in India,* Vol. 2, New Delhi: Wildlife Trust of India.

Sekhsaria, P. (2009), 'When *Chanos cChanos* became *Tsunami Macchi*: The Post-December 2004 Scenario in the Andaman and Nicobar Islands', *Journal of the Bombay Natural History Society,* 106(3), 256–62.

Singh, S.S. (2006), *The Nicobar Islands: Cultural Choices in the Aftermath of the Tsunami,* Vienna: Oliver Lehmann.

Sivakumar, K. (2006), 'Wildlife and Tsunami: A Rapid Assessment on the Impact of Tsunami on the Nicobar Megapode and Other Associated Coastal Species in the Nicobar Group of Islands – Summary Report', Dehradun: Wildlife Institute of India.

Thakkar, M.G. and B. Goyal (2006), Historic Submergence and Tsunami Destruction of Nancowrie, Camorta, Katchall and Trinket Islands of Nicobar District: Consequences of 26 December 2004 Sumatra-Andaman Earthquake', *Current Science,* 90(7), 989–94.

Verma, N. (2012), 'Address by Admiral Nirmal Verma Chief of Naval Staff, on the Commissionng of INS Baaz (NAS

CAMPBELL BAY)'. http://ajaishukla.blogspot.in/2012/07/ins-baaz-indian-navys-air-station-in.html (accessed on 13 May 2013).

Wild Life Protection Act, Government of India, 1972 (Amended 2006).

Zafar-ul-Islam, M. and A. Rahmani (eds) (2004), *Important Bird Areas in India: Priority Sites for Conservation*, Mumbai: Indian Bird Conservation Network; Bombay Natural History Society; and Edinburgh, UK: Birdlife International.

25

TRIBAL RESERVES, IBAs AND BIRD CONSERVATION: THE UNIQUE CASE OF THE ANDAMAN AND NICOBAR ISLANDS

Indian Birds, 2013

Introduction

THE ANDAMAN AND NICOBAR Islands are a small group of about 570 islands in the Bay of Bengal spread over an area of roughly 8,200 sq. km (Jayaraj and Andrews, 2005). They occupy only about 0.25 per cent of the total landmass of India but are disproportionately rich in endemism and diversity. Pande et al. (2007) have noted, quoting Sankaran and Vijayan (1993) and Vijayan et al. (2000): '103–105 taxa (37–38.2 per cent) out of 268–270 avian species and races recorded from these islands are endemic – illustrating a high degree of endemism.'

The islands have also been designated as two of the 221 major Endemic Bird Areas (EBAs) of the world – EBA 125 (Andaman Islands) and EBA 126 (Nicobar Islands) where the restricted range species reported from the Andamans and the Nicobars are thirteen and nine respectively (Stattersfield et al. 1998). Jathar and Rahmani (2006), however, note that twenty-eight endemic bird species (excluding races) are reported from these islands – twenty are endemic to the Andamans, and eight to the Nicobars. The two data-deficient bird species from India listed in the *Red Data Book* of the IUCN are also found in these islands: the Andaman crake *Rallina canningi* and the Nicobar scops-owl *Otus alius* (Table 9). It is evident that the islands are important for bird conservation and this is reflected in the fact that they have nineteen areas that have been identified as Important Bird Areas (IBAs) by Zafar-ul-Islam and Rahmani (2004) (Table 7)

IBAs and Tribal Reserves

Of particular significance in the context of the Andaman and Nicobar Islands are forest areas designated as tribal reserves under the Andaman and Nicobar Protection of Aboriginal Tribes Regulation (ANPATR), 1956 (amended in 2004). This includes the entire group of the Nicobar Islands (about 1,900 sq. km) and four tribal reserves in the Andaman Islands that cover nearly 1,600 sq. km of some of the most pristine forests that still survive here. In the Andamans, these tribal reserves are named after the four aboriginal communities that have been living in these islands for at least 40,000 years: the Great Andamanese, the Jarawas, the Onge and the Sentinelese.

Six of the nineteen IBAs in the islands are areas designated as tribal reserves under the ANPATR. These include the islands of Car Nicobar, Great Nicobar, Little Nicobar, Tillangchong, Camorta, Katchal, Nancowry and Trinket: all in the Nicobar Islands (Table 7).

Tribal Reserves in the Andaman Islands

The tribal reserves in the Andamans are the last remaining large and contiguous areas of the original giant evergreen, Andaman evergreen and the southern tropical evergreen rainforests that these islands are reputed for. The reserves are, in fact, more significant and important for biodiversity conservation than wildlife sanctuaries and national parks (the protected area network) of the islands (Table 8) (Pande et al. 1991; Kutty and Kothari 2001; WLPA 1972 [Amended 2006]; Anon. 2011b). While the terrestrial ecosystem under the protected area network in the Andaman Islands is only about 500 sq. km, the total forest areas under the tribal reserve cover is more than three times the figure, at 1,600 sq. km.

The Jarawa Tribal Reserve alone is spread over an area of a little more than 1,000 sq. km of tropical forests (Sekhsaria and Pandya 2010; ANPATR 2004 [1956]), whereas the Onge Tribal Reserve covers 520 sq. km. of contiguous forests in Little Andaman Island (Sekhsaria 2004b; ANPATR 2004 [1956]). Studies and satellite images have shown that some of the best forests and biological diversity in these islands now survive mainly inside the boundaries of these tribal reserves (Table 8).

The Forests outside Tribal Reserves

Large areas located outside these Andaman tribal reserves
have experienced logging that has gone on for almost a
century. These forests, with the small exception of the
protected area network, have either become deciduous
because of timber extraction that has gone on for almost a
century, or have been completely denuded to be converted to
agricultural fields, horticultural plantations or settlements of
large numbers of immigrants from mainland India (Saldanha
1989; Andrews 2002; Chandi 2002; Singh 2002; IIRS 2003,
Sekhsaria 2003; Chandi and Andrews 2010; Sekhsaria and
Pandya 2010).

Forests within the present protected area network have
also seen logging in the past. The case of the Interview Island
Wildlife Sanctuary, which is also an IBA, is an illustrative
one. This is the largest contiguous forest stretch in the
Andamans that is protected under the provisions of the
Wild Life Protection Act. The area, however, is only 133 sq.
km (Pande et al. 1991; Anon. 2011b) as compared to the
little over 1,000 sq. km. that constitutes the Jarawa Tribal
Reserve. Significantly, the forests of Interview Island were
under commercial extraction from the 1950s till about mid-
1960s (Pande et al. 1991), while a major area of the Jarawa
Reserve Forest has never seen any logging operations.

Conservation Implications

The implications for conservation are evident in other ways
as well. Not only is the total area protected under tribal
reserves much larger, the individual area in a majority of

the protected areas is extremely small: fifty-eight of the protected areas are less than 1 sq. km in area each and only four have an area of more than 30 sq. km (Davidar et al. 1995). Davidar et al. (1995) also found a direct relationship between presence of butterfly and bird species and size of the forest area studied, particularly in the case of isolated islands. Many species of birds were not recorded at all on small islands and all forest bird species were only found on islands larger than 30 sq. km.

Where avifauna, in particular, is concerned, it is striking that all but one of the species in the Andaman group of islands that are endemic or listed as either data-deficient or near-threatened in the IBA directory (Zafar-ul-Islam and Rahmani 2004) can be found in these tribal reserves (Table 9). The only exception is the Narcondam hornbill *Aceros narcondami*, but that is an extraordinary situation in any case. Even other significant species like the Andaman teal *Anas albogularis* and beach thick-knee *Esacus magnirostris* have been reported from the tribal reserves (Vijayan et al. 2006; Rahmani 2012). The conservation significance with regard to the Nicobars is that the entire group is a tribal reserve!

A recent preliminary assessment also shows, for instance, that the resource basket of the Jarawas consists of more than 100 species of plants and animals, a third of which are edible (Kumar et al. 2010). This is an important indicator of the knowledge the Jarawas themselves have as also of the diversity that the forests of the Jarawa Reserve support. It is extremely significant because this is bound to be a very important knowledge source in a forest landscape that has hardly been explored and studied in the context of modern science.

The Historical Context of the Andamans

Also important to understand are the changes that have occurred in the recent past in these islands in general, and in the Andamans in particular. The most important indicator of the changes is the population figure. While the estimated population of the four indigenous communities in the Andamans was about 700 individuals in the census of 1961, it came down to a little more than 400 individuals in 2001. Of these, the Onges and the Jarawas were reported to be ninety-six and 240 individuals respectively, and the Sentinelese population was estimated to be only thirty-nine (Tables 3 and 4).

At the same time, the total population in the Andaman group increased from a little less than 50,000 individuals in 1961 to over 350,000 in 2001 (Pandit 1990; Anon. 2001). This increase in population was based almost entirely on an official policy of the Government of India to promote immigration from mainland India to 'colonize' these islands (Anonymous 1965). Within a period of five decades, the total number of non-indigenous people in the Andamans had gone up from seventy per indigenous individual to 751 per aboriginal individual (Sekhsaria and Pandya 2010). The demand for resources like land, forests and water was bound to increase proportionately.

De-notification of the Tribal Reserves

Related directly to this influx of people into the islands was the process of the de-notification of large areas from under the tribal reserve category, particularly in the 1970s. A series of amendments to the ANPATR in 1972, 1973, 1977 and 1979 resulted in the removal of Rutland Island (103 sq. km) from the category of tribal reserve, nearly 200 sq. km. from the Onge Tribal Reserve in Little Andaman, and 300 sq. km from the Jarawa Tribal Reserve in South Andaman (Anon. 1976; ANPATR 2004 [1956]) (see Map 3 in Chapter 8).

Large areas of these de-notified tribal reserve forests were then clear-felled for the housing, agricultural and horticultural needs of the settlers. Work was started on the construction of the Andaman Trunk Road (ATR) that was to cut through the heart of the Jarawa Tribal Reserve as it sought to connect Port Blair in South Andaman Island to Diglipur in North Andaman Island. The de-notification of the tribal reserves coupled with the construction of the ATR facilitated intensive logging in these forests as is evident from timber extraction statistics. The 1980s consistently saw an annual average of 14,000 cu. m of timber extraction from the Andaman forests (Saldanha 1989; Singh 2002; Anonymous 2005) (Table 2 in Chapter 2). This was at the cost of the rights and integrity of the aboriginal communities as well as the biological diversity of these islands.

The impact and implications of this can well be imagined, and this is reflected in the site accounts that we see in the IBA directory (Zafar-ul-Islam and Rahmani 2004) as well. Population increase, habitat fragmentation, encroachments and poaching have been identified as the main threats and problems in the context of IBAs and avifauna conservation in the islands.

Supreme Court Orders of 2002

Many of these issues were dealt with in the orders passed
by the Supreme Court of India in 2002 in response to a
public interest litigation (Intervention Application [IA]-502,
2002) filed by non-governmental organizations (Appendices
I and II). The court had asked for the implementation of
an inner line area system to prevent the influx of people
from mainland India, for commercial timber extraction to
be stopped, for removal of encroachments, phasing out of
sand mining from the island's beaches, use of appropriate
construction materials, closure of the Andaman and Nicobar
Forest Plantation and Development Corporation that had
been logging the forests of Little and Middle Andaman since
the 1970s, and for closure of the ATR where it runs through
and along the forests in the Jarawa Reserve (Sekhsaria 2003;
Singh 2002; IA-502 2002).

More than a decade later, many of these orders are yet to
be implemented. The member of parliament for the islands
has even argued for the de-notification of the JTR and to
make the land and forests available for development (Anon.
2010a). In a meeting in 2012 with Manmohan Singh, the then
prime minister of India, members of the Andaman Chamber
of Commerce and Industry were reported to have questioned
the justification of setting aside the Jarawa Tribal Reserve as
an area seven times the size of the city of Chennai for only
about 300 Jarawas (Anon. 2012).

The Case of Tillangchong Island in the Nicobars

The dilemmas and the challenges faced are starkly highlighted in other recent developments, related this time to the uninhabited Tillangchong Island spread over 17 sq. km in the Nicobars. The island is an important population repository of the Nicobari megapode *Megapodius nicobariensis,* the race endemic to the Nancowry subgroup of islands (Sivakumar 2010); *Megapodius nicobariensis abbotti* is endemic to the southern Great Nicobar group of islands. The island is a wildlife sanctuary (Pande et al. 1991; Kutty and Kothari 2001), a tribal reserve (ANPATR 2004), an IBA (Zafar-ul-Islam and Rahmani 2004), and of great customary and ritual importance for the Nicobari tribal community (Chandi 2012). Yet, in November 2011, the Indian Navy thought it right to go ahead and seek permission to construct a temporary missile testing range on this small but culturally and ecologically important island (Chandi 2012; Anon. 2011a).

It was only in late 2012, after a sustained campaign in the media, particularly by wildlife and environmental NGOs, that the Ministry of Environment and Forests of the Government of India issued an order (Khanduri 2012) rejecting the proposal on grounds of the 'high conservation values' of the place. Not only had the wildlife and biodiversity value of the place been given short shrift in the proposal, the laws and regulations related to tribal rights had also been ignored.

Conclusion

We have, in the Andaman and Nicobar Islands, a unique situation and opportunity where the protection of the indigenous peoples, the forests and the biodiversity including its rich avifauna are all intricately linked. Ensuring protection of the tribal reserves will, for instance, not only ensure the survival of the increasingly threatened indigenous communities of these islands like the Jarawas and the Onge but also bring significant other benefits. Protection in these areas simply cannot be divorced from the future of the indigenous peoples. Safeguarding the rights, culture and society of the indigenous people might be the best and most effective method of protecting the forests and biodiversity and avifauna as well. This, as we have seen, is far easier said than done, and a number of steps are needed to achieve this:

a) Scientific research: The forests of the tribal reserves in these islands remain unstudied and unexplored from a scientific point of view. A larger and coordinated effort is needed to uncover the biological richness of these forests in an effort to strengthen the case for their conservation and protection.

b) Working with the settler communities: While the indigenous communities have the primary right to the forests and the resources, it has to be borne in mind that a much larger number of outsiders now live along and around the forests of the tribal reserves. These comprise the first line of interaction with the forests and the indigenous communities themselves. A concerted effort needs to be made to engage with them and educate them on the rights of these communities and on the richness and importance of these forests alongside benefits such as fresh water and other ecosystem services that they derive from these forests.

c) Implementation of Supreme Court orders: Supreme Court orders of 2002 (Singh 2002; Sekhsaria 2003) need to be implemented in letter and spirit as a step towards respecting the rights and territorial integrity of communities like the Jarawa, and in the larger interest of forest protection and biodiversity conservation in the islands.

Table 7: List of IBAs in the Andaman and Nicobar Islands (Zafar-ul-Islam and Rahmani, 2004)

IBA site code	IBA site name
IN-AN-01	Austin Strait
IN-AN-02	Baratang-Rafters Creek
IN-AN-03	Car Nicobar
IN-AN-04	Chaipur and Hanspuri
IN-AN-05	Great Nicobar, Little Nicobar
IN-AN-06	Interview Island Wildlife Sanctuary
IN-AN-07	Jarawa Reserve (Middle Andaman and South Andaman)
IN-AN-08	Kadakachang
IN-AN-09	Landfall Island Wildlife Sanctuary
IN-AN-10	Little Andaman
IN-AN-11	Mahatma Gandhi Marine National Park
IN-AN-12	Mount Diavalo/Cuthbert Bay
IN-AN-13	Mount Harriet National Park
IN-AN-14	Narcondam Island Wildlife Sanctuary
IN-AN-15	North and South Sentinel
IN-AN-16	North Reef Island Wildlife Sanctuary
IN-AN-17	Rani Jhansi Marine National Park
IN-AN-18	Saddle Peak National Park
IN-AN-19	Tillangchong, Camorta, Katchal, Nancowry and Trinket

d) Additional legal protection for tribal reserves: Measures to provide additional legal protection to these tribal reserves – for instance, under the provisions of the 2006 law that seeks to correct historical wrongs and gives rights to scheduled tribes and forest dwellers (The Schediled Tribes and Other Traditional Forest Dwellers [Recognition of Forest Rights] Act, commonly known as the Forest Rights Act, 2006) – need to be explored urgently. It is only when all, or at least some of these steps, are initiated in these islands that the interests of indigenous communities and those of biodiversity conservation will be achieved.

Table 8: Protection accorded to the forests in the Andaman Islands: Total area of the Andamans: 6,408 sq. km

Particulars	Sanctuaries and National Parks	Tribal Reserves
Total number	99 (92 sanctuaries and 7 national parks)	4
Forest areas protected	c. 500 sq. km	c.1,600 sq. km
Percentage total forest area	8%	20%
Marine areas protected	c. 500 sq. km	c. 1,000 sq. km
Largest forest area protected	Interview Island Sanctuary (133 sq. km)	Jarawa Reserve (c. 1,000 sq. km)

TRIBAL RESERVES, IBAS... 197

Table 9: *Red Data Book* and endemic species

VULNERABLE
Narcondam hornbill *Aceros narcondami*

DATA DEFICIENT
Andaman crake *Rallina canningi*

NEAR THREATENED
Andaman serpent eagle *Spilornis elgini*
Andaman wood pigeon *Columba palumboides*
Andaman cuckoo dove *Macropygia rufipennis*
Andaman scops owl *Otus balli*
Andaman hawk owl *Ninox affinis*
Andaman black woodpecker *Dryocopus hodgei*
Andaman drongo *Dicrurus andamanensis*
Andaman tree pie *Dendrocitta bayleyi*

OTHER ENDEMIC SPECIES
Andaman coucal *Centropus andamanensis*
White-headed starling *Sturnus erythropygius*

Source: Zafar-ul-Islam and Rahmani, 2004

References

Andrews, H. (2002), 'Impact Assessment around the Jarawa Reserve, Middle and South Andaman Islands', in Mukhopadhyay K., R.K. Bhattacharya and B.N. Sarkar (eds), *Jarawa Contact – ours with them, theirs with us*, Kolkata: Anthropological Survey of India.

Anon. (1965), 'Report by the Inter Departmental Team on Accelerated Development Program for A&N Islands', New Delhi: Ministry of Rehabilitation, Government of India.

Anon. (1976), 'Project Report for Logging, Marketing, Forest Plantation and Natural Regeneration in Little Andaman and North Andaman Islands', Port Blair: Andaman and Nicobar

Islands Forest Plantation and Development Corporation (ANFPDC) Ltd.

Anon. (2001), *Census of India*, Port Blair: Government of India.

Anon. (2005), *Forest Statistics,* Port Blair: Andaman and Nicobar Islands Forest Department, Andaman and Nicobar Administration.

Anon (2010a), 'Bishnu submits agenda points for consideration of Standing Committee meeting of IDA', http://in.groups.yahoo.com/group/andamanicobar/message/6551 (accessed on 14 September 2011).

Anon. (2010b), 'Jarawa population rises to 375', http://in.groups.yahoo.com/group/andamanicobar/message/7183 (accessed on 14 September 2011).

Anon. (2011a), 'Navy's Andaman & Nicobar Missile Test Plan Hits Green Hurdle' *The Times of India*, 9 November 2011.

Anon. (2011b), 'Protected Area Network in India', New Delhi, http://moef.nic.in (accessed on 2 February 2012).

Anon. (2012), 'ACCI Delegation Discuss ATR, Buffer Zone Issue with the Prime Minister', *The Daily Telegrams*, 18 January 2012.

ANPATR (2004), Andaman and Nicobar Protection of Aboriginal Tribes Regulation Including all Amendments till 2004, No. 4 CFR, India: Andaman & Nicobar Administration (1956).

Chakraborty T. (2010), 'Jarawas Add 125 to Tribe', Kolkata, 17 October 2010, http://www.telegraphindia.com/1101017/jsp/nation/story_13066500.jsp (accessed on 29 February 2012).

Chandi, M. (2002), 'Territory and landscape around the Jarawa Reserve', in Mukhopadhyay K., R.K. Bhattacharya and B.N. Sarkar (eds), *Jarawa contact – ours with them, theirs with us.* Kolkata: Anthropological Survey of India

—— (2012), 'Targeting Tillangchong', *The Hindu Sunday Magazine*, Chennai, 22 January 2012.

Chandi M. and Andrews H. (2010), 'The Jarawa Tribal Reserve: The "last" Andaman forest', in Sekhsaria P. and Pandya V., (eds), *The Jarawa Tribal Reserve Dossier: cultural and biological diversities in the Andaman Islands*, Paris: UNESCO and Pune: Kalpavriksh.

Davidar P., S. Devi, T.R.K. Yoganand and T. Ganesh (1995), 'Reserve Size and Implications for the Conservation of Biodiversity in the Andaman Islands', in Boyle T.J.B. and B. Boontawee (eds), *Measuring and Monitoring Biodiversity in Tropical and Temperate Forests*, Jakarta: CIFOR.

IA-502 (2002), Intervention Application 502 in WP (C) No. 202/1995. *T.N. Thirumalpad Vs Union of India and Ors* (Supreme Court of India, 2002).

IIRS (2003), *Biodiversity Characterization at Landscape Levels in the Andaman and Nicobar Islands using Satellite Remote Sensing and Geographic Information System*, Dehradun: Indian Institute of Remote Sensing, Department of Space, Government of India.

Jathar, G.A. and Rahmani, A.R. (2006), 'Endemic Birds of India', *Buceros*, 11 (2 & 3): 1–53.

Jayaraj, R. and Andrews, H. (eds) (2005), *Andaman and Nicobar Islands Union Territory Biodiversity Strategy and Action Plan*, Port Blair: Andaman and Nicobar Administration.

Khanduri, S.K. (2012), Office Memorandum – Permission for erection of structure within Tillangchong Sanctuary, Andaman and Nicobar Islands for temporary use by Indian navy, reg. in: DIVISION, M.O.E.A.F.W. (ed.), New Delhi: Government of India.

Kumar, U., B.N. Sarkar, K. Mukhopadhyay, K. M. Sinha Roy, R. Sahani, and S.S. Dutta Chowdhury (2010), 'The Jarawas and their lands', in P. Sekhsaria and V. Pandya (eds), *The Jarawa Tribal Reserve Dossier: Cultural and biological diversities in the Andaman Islands*, Paris: UNESCO; Pune: Kalpavriksh.

Kutty, R. and A. Kothari, (eds) (2001), *Protected Areas in India: A profile*, Pune: Kalpavriksh.

Pande, P., A. Kothari, and S. Singh, (eds) (1991), *Directory of National Parks and Sanctuaries in Andaman and Nicobar Islands: Management status and profiles*, New Delhi: Indian

Institute of Public Administration.

Pande, S., N. Sant, S. Ranade, S. Pednekar, P. Mestry, P. Deshpande, S. Kharat and V. Deshmukh (2007), 'Avifaunal survey of Andaman and Nicobar Islands', *Indian Birds*, 3 (5), 8 January 2007, pp. 162–80.

Pandit, T.N. (1990), *The Sentinelese*, Kolkata: Anthropological Survey of India and Seagull Books.

Rahmani, A.R. (2012), *Threatened Birds of India: Their conservation requirements*, Mumbai: Indian Bird Conservation Network, Bombay Natural History Society, Royal Society for the Protection of Birds, BirdLife International, Oxford University Press, pp. i–xvi, 1–864.

Saldanha, C.J. (1989), *Andaman, Nicobar and Lakshadweep: An environmental impact assessment*, New Delhi: Oxford & IBH Publishing Co. Pvt. Ltd.

Sankaran, R. and L. Vijayan (1993), 'The Avifauna of the Andaman and Nicobar Islands: A Review and the Current Scenario', in A. Verghese, S. Sridhar and A.K. Chakravarthy (eds), *Bird Conservation: Strategies for the Nineties and Beyond*, Bangalore: Ornithological Society of India, pp. 255–71.

Sekhsaria, P. (2003), *Troubled Islands: Writings on the Indigenous peoples and environment of the Andaman & Nicobar Islands*, New Delhi: LEAD India; Pune: Kalpavriksh.

—— (2004a), 'IBAs and Tribal Reserves: The unique situation in the Andaman and Nicobar Islands', *Mistnet*, Vol. 5, Nos 3 & 4, Mumbai: Bombay Natural History Society.

—— (2004b), 'Illegal Logging and Deforestation in Andaman and Nicobar Islands, India: The Story of Little Andaman', *Journal of Sustainable Forestry*, Vol. 19, pp. 319–35.

—— (2009), 'When *Chanos chanos* Became Tsunami Macchi: The post-December 2004 Scenario in the Andaman and Nicobar Islands', *Journal of the Bombay Natural History Society*, 106 (3), pp. 256–62.

Sekhsaria, P. and Pandya, V. (eds) (2010), *The Jarawa Tribal Reserve Dossier: Cultural and biological diversities in the Andaman*

Islands. Paris: UNESCO; Pune: Kalpavriksh.

Singh, S. (2002), *Report of the Commission set up under the orders of the Supreme Court on the Status of the Forests and other Allied Matters in Andaman and Nicobar Islands*, New Delhi: Indian Institute of Public Administration.

Sivakumar, K. (2010), 'Impact of tsunami on the Nicobar megapode *Megopodius nicobariensis*', *Oryx*, Vol. 44, pp. 71–78.

Stattersfield, A. J., M.J. Crosby, M.J. Long and D.C. Wege (1998), *Endemic Bird Areas of the World: Priorities for biodiversity conservation*, Cambridge, UK: BirdLife International, pp. 1–846.

Vijayan, L., R. Sankaran, K. Sivakumar and V. Murugan (2000), *A study on the ecology, status and conservation perspectives of certain rare endemic avifauna of the Andaman and Nicobar Islands: Final Report*, Coimbatore: Salim Ali Centre for Ornithology and Natural History.

Vijayan, L., V. Murugan and M.A.R. Mamannan (2006), 'Conservation of Andaman Teal', *TWSG News*, No. 15, pp. 55–59.

WLPA 1972 (Amended 2006), Wild Life (Protection) Act, India. (2006).

Zafar-ul-Islam M. and Rahmani, A.R. (2004), *Important Bird Areas in India: Priority sites for conservation*, 1st edition, Mumbai: Indian Bird Conservation Network; Bombay Natural History Society and Edinburg, UK: Bird Life International, pp. i–xviii, 1–1133.

APPENDICES

RECOMMENDATIONS OF THE SHEKHAR SINGH COMMISSION,[1] JANUARY 2002

A. Commercial forestry

Recommendations

Forest harvesting

1) Felling of trees and collection of non-timber forest produce (NTFP) should be banned from the forests of Little Andaman Island and all tribal reserves except for i) collection of NTFP from already worked forests of Little Andaman and from forest areas designated for the purpose in the Nicobar group of islands, for meeting the legitimate consumption of local inhabitants; ii) collection of timber and other forest produce by tribals living within tribal reserves for meeting their bona fide needs.

2) Harvesting of all forest produce including timber and

---

[1] Appointed by the Supreme Court in November 2001.

NTFP should be completely prohibited from national parks and sanctuaries.

3)   In addition to areas covered under 1 and 2 above, no felling of trees should be allowed in any unworked forest area, i.e., area where felling of trees as per working plans, working schemes, felling schemes or approved working plans has not taken place earlier. There should also be no diversion of forestland from any such unworked area or from areas covered under 1 and 2 above, without the specific orders of the Supreme Court.

4)   No felling of trees for whatsoever reasons or justification should be carried out to supply to, or to meet the raw material requirement of plywood, veneer, block board, match stick or any other such wood-based units except to local small-scale units (including sawmills) solely for meeting the local requirement for sawn timber and other wood-based products.

5)   For meeting the timber and other forest produce requirements of inhabitants of the Andaman and Nicobar Islands (ANI), felling of trees from forest areas not covered under 1, 2 and 3 above, i.e., forest area worked earlier in accordance with working plans, working schemes, felling schemes or approved working plans and excluding areas falling within national parks, sanctuaries, tribal reserves or Little Andaman may be allowed. Such felling may be undertaken as per prescriptions of the working plans approved by the MoEF. These plans should also contain action plans for removing, in a phased manner, trees of commercial species that are in number or concentration in excess of what is found in a natural forest of the same type and similar location. Concurrently, efforts should

be made to bring back the forest to its natural profile by encouraging/reintroducing those species of fauna and flora that naturally occurred in these forests prior to their being 'converted'. The working plan should also contain sufficient provisions for regeneration of felled areas. In accordance with an earlier Supreme Court order of 22 September 2000, felling of trees should be allowed only if sufficient financial provisions for implementing the working plan prescriptions have been made.

6) In the meanwhile, the present ban on felling of trees may be continued and the local requirement of timber and other forest produce may be met by utilizing the already felled trees and sawn timber lying with the forest department and the Andaman and Nicobar Islands Forest Plantation and Development Corporation Ltd. (ANIFPDC).

7) Once the stock of already felled trees and sawn timber is depleted, the local requirement of timber should be met, as far as possible, by harvesting the monoculture and mixed plantations of padauk, gurjan, teak and other species. The felling of trees from already worked natural forests, as specified in 5 above, should be undertaken only to meet the balance requirement. However, if the local requirement of timber and other forest produce is more than what could be obtained by felling of plantations and sustainably extracting trees from worked areas, as specified in 5 above, the same may be met by bringing timber in from other parts of the country. Under no circumstances should the over-harvesting of the forest available for felling under para 5 above be permitted or undertaken.

8) There should be no expansion of monoculture or commercial plantations on forestland. The existing plantations of oil palm, rubber and teak are reportedly no longer viable and should be phased out. The land so released should, in so far as it is forestland, be regenerated as specified earlier. Consequently, the ANIFPDC should be wound up as it was primarily set up to promote commercial forestry and plantations, especially in Little Andaman.

9) At the same time, efforts should be made to reduce the level of demand for timber and firewood. For the purpose, the A&N Administration should investigate and implement methods of achieving this, including the conversion to the wood and bamboo-based 'Assam type' construction, which is both less timber intensive, and safer in earthquakes, than the present all-timber or RCC buildings.

Wood-based Industry

10) There should be a complete ban on the establishment of any new wood-based unit for the next ten years.

11) All existing small-scale wood-based units (sawmills) should be relocated within industrial estates or, where industrial estates are not feasible, in locations contiguous to forest offices or otherwise convenient for the forest department to monitor. This relocation should be completed within one year, after which the non-complying saw mills should be closed down. These saw mills should also be required to obtain a licence from the ANI Forest Department within three months and to

maintain such records as may be prescribed by the forest department. Their licence may be renewed every year at the discretion of the ANI Forest Department, after the department has satisfied itself that a) the unit was not involved in the use of any illegal timber; b) the prescribed records were properly maintained; c) all provisions of the act, rules and the terms and conditions stipulated by the forest department from time to time have been complied with. Necessary rules, guidelines etc., for the purpose, should be prescribed by the forest department within three months.

12) No subsidy of any type, including transport subsidy, should be given to any wood-based unit.

13) Existing medium and large-scale wood-based industries (including plywood, veneer and match industries) can be allowed to function provided they import their entire requirement of wood and other forest-based raw materials from the mainland or from abroad. No subsidies should be allowed to them.

14) No timber, either as logs or as sawn timber or plywood/ veneer, or in any other form, should be transported out of the islands through any means whatsoever. This should not, however, inhibit the transportation, as personal baggage, of a reasonable quantity of wooden handicrafts by tourists or of personal articles by those permanently leaving the islands. Also, where a wood-based industry, as specified in 13 above, imports its entire wood and forest-based raw material requirement, then it should be permitted to export its finished product.

B. Using untreated timber for construction

Recommendation

15) All timber, bamboo and cane used for construction and requiring treatment in order to extend its durability and life, should be so treated and the administration should ensure that requisite capacity to treat all such timber is in position within a period of six months. After the expiry of this period, no timber, bamboo or cane of the type requiring treatment should be sold for use in building and construction activities, or used for such purpose, unless it has been appropriately treated.

C. Encroachments

Recommendations

16) Any further regularization of encroachments on forestland in any form, including allotment/use of forestland for agricultural or horticultural purposes, should be strictly prohibited.

17) All those families who have been identified as having encroached on forestland prior to 1978 and have not yet shifted to their allotted rehabilitation sites, should be given three months' notice to vacate their encroachments and shift to the allotted land. Failing this, their allotment should be cancelled and they should be forcibly evicted within three months of the deadline being over, without any further claim to land or any other form of rehabilitation.

18) Similarly, those among the pre-1978 families who have

shifted to their allotted sites but have occupied more land than they were entitled to should also be given three months' notice to vacate the extra land occupied by them. On the expiry of this notice period, the allotments of those who have not complied with this notice should be cancelled and they should be forcibly evicted within three months, without any further claim to compensation or land.

19) All post-1978 forest encroachments should be completely removed forthwith and, in any case, within six months. Post-1978 encroachers (except for foreign nationals) should be allotted homesteads in revenue land and training and opportunity for self-employment or for other types of livelihood activities provided.

20) The forest officials in the ANI should be given requisite powers to do this, including:

- Power of summary eviction of encroachments: As in the case of Madhya Pradesh, vide Section 80A, IFA, 1927.

- Magisterial powers to assistant conservators of forests: Assistant Conservators of Forests should be appointed as executive magistrates/special executive magistrates in order to oversee the evictions carried out by the Range Officers on receipt of orders of eviction from the estate officers.

21) For the purpose, an effective action plan should be prepared and implemented under direct supervision, monitoring and control of a committee comprising the Lt. Governor, Chief Secretary, Principal Chief Conservator of Forests of ANI, and reputed local NGO representatives. The Chief Secretary, ANI, may be asked

to file a monthly progress report in the Supreme Court.

22) In order to prevent any further encroachments and rampant immigration, the administration should, within three months, regulate the entry of people to the islands by having the islands declared as an inner line area and by imposing relevant restrictions under Section 3 and other provisions of the Environment (Protection) Act of 1986. In accordance with this, non-residents entering the islands should have to invariably register themselves so that those who do not return to the mainland within reasonable time can be traced and, where they have illegally encroached on land, can be evicted from these encroachments at the earliest. In addition, entry to the more vulnerable and forested areas of the islands should be restricted.

23) Once this regulation is in position, the administration should, in a time-bound manner, issue identity cards to all the residents so that there is no gap in the period of identification and issuance of ID cards. This would ensure that fresh illegal encroachers are easily identified. Subsidized travel to the islands should, once identity cards have been issued, be available only to bona fide residents of the islands.

24) Divisional Forest Officers and, where relevant, village protection committees, as described later, should be made responsible for prevention, early detection and quick eviction of new forest encroachers.

25) The forest department should be strengthened and appropriate village institutions set up for the purpose, as detailed later.

D. Road through the Jarawa Tribal Reserve

Recommendation

26) The Andaman Trunk Road (ATR) should be closed to all vehicular traffic from Miletilak in South Andaman to the northern boundary of the S. Andaman Island. Similarly, it should be closed to all traffic from Kadamtala (corresponding to Prolobjig camp No.3) in Middle Andaman up to Kaushalya Nagar (corresponding to Porlobjig camp No. 15). This should be done within three months. Further, no person except for the Jarawas living in the Reserve should be allowed to enter the Reserve by any means unless he/she is permitted by the Principal Chief Conservator of Forests, and the Secretary, Tribal Welfare, ANI administration, and no such permission should be granted unless the person is proceeding on bona fide work related to the welfare of the tribals or the protection of the area.

E. Diversion of land and felling of trees for development projects and activities

Recommendations

27) The felling of 27 trees for the 33 KV transmission line from Bamboo Flat to Minnie Bay and 17 trees for construction of rural road from Adajig to Flat Bay Village should be permitted as a one-time relaxation, as these projects are already in their final stages, a small number of trees are involved and, reportedly, necessary clearances had been obtained from the MoEF prior to the Supreme

Court's order of 10 January 2001. However, all other proposals or clearances under the Forest (Conservation) Act of 1980 or the Environment (Protection) Act of 1986, where diversion of land or felling of trees or other activities that would have an impact on the environment, are still to be undertaken, should be put up for review by the Supreme Court.

28) For the conservation and protection of the forests and other ecosystems, an effective action plan should be prepared by the ANI Forest Department, in consultation with local NGOs and experts. This plan should also envisage a suitable enhancement of the protected area network, especially in the main islands of the Andaman and in the Nicobar Group. All unworked forest areas in Diglipur, Mayabundar, Middle Andamans and Baratang should be made into national parks, leaving a buffer belt between the national park boundary and the edge of revenue settlements, for protection by village protection committees. In addition, there should be a consolidation of the nearly 100 small island parks and sanctuaries and they should be constituted into viable units encompassing the marine areas surrounding them. This plan, after being approved by the MoEF, should be strictly implemented. The necessary funds, vehicles, equipment, human power, police help and legal power required for the effective implementation of this action plan should be made available by the ANI administration.

29) Appropriate regulations under existing Acts like the Environment (Protection) Act of 1986, with similar objectives as The Delhi Preservation of Trees Act, 1994, currently in force in the Union Territory of Delhi, should

be set in place in ANI, within six months, to regulate the felling of trees on non-forest land.

F. Poaching

Recommendations

30) The forest department should be immediately strengthened in order to be able to effectively prevent poaching.
31) Forest officers should be given adequate powers, under the Indian Forest Act of 1927 (IFA,) as has been done in other states, to meet the threat of poaching. These could include:
    - Power of confiscation: as provided for vide Section 52, 52A, 52B and 52C IFA, 1927 in Bihar, Section 52A and 52B in Himachal Pradesh, Section 52, 52A, 52B, and 52C in Madhya Pradesh, Section 62A to 61G of Goa, Section 61a to Section 62G of Gujarat, and Section 61A to 61G of Maharashtra.
    - Increase in the limit fixed for amount of compensation for trees under Section 68(3) IFA, 1927: The present limit of ₹50 is required to be increased to ₹10,000 as in Goa.
32) A co-ordination mechanism should be set up where the forest department, the civil administration, the Coast Guard and the Combined Defence Command in ANI can take co-ordinated action against poachers, especially against foreign poachers.

G. Introduction of exotics

Recommendations

33) No exotic species of fauna or flora should be introduced into the islands. Accordingly, a suitable set of guidelines and procedures should be developed for the purpose.

34) A time-bound action plan should be drawn up to deal with the exotics already on the island, including weeds, and their removal/eradication should be taken up on a war footing, including the translocation of elephants back to the mainland and the inhibition of breeding, by deer, by darting the alpha males with anti-fertility drugs, as has been successfully tried in other countries.

H. Collection and distribution of royalty-free timber and non-timber forest produce

Recommendations

35) The practice of distributing timber and NTFP free to settlers should be discontinued. Instead, rural populations should be formed into village forest protection committees and, as per the joint forest protection norms prevalent in other parts of the country, the amount of timber and NTFP required by village communities should be given to them on the basis of a memorandum of understanding, in return for their role in protecting the forests adjacent to their settlements and in detecting and preventing encroachments.

36) Government departments, including defence and PWD, should be supplied fuel wood and other required forest

produce by the forest department and should not be permitted to directly collect these from the forests.

37) Concurrent efforts should be made to minimize demand for forest-based resources. The administration should encourage the use of sawdust as fuel, as is the practice in many other parts of the country. They should also investigate the possibility of replacing firewood as a domestic fuel by gas and consider giving a one-time subsidy for the purchase of gas stoves and cylinders to the poor rural population. Adequate supply of LPG to the islands should be ensured on a priority basis.

I. Mining of sand

Recommendations

38) The extraction of sand should be phased out and no further extension should be granted after the current extension is over on 30 September 2002.

39) As already mentioned earlier, alternate material for construction, including treated bamboo and soft woods, should be encouraged as this is less damaging to the environment and safer in case of an earthquake. Stone dust should be utilized where use of concrete is essential.

J. Inappropriate tourism

Recommendations

40) No concrete or permanent infrastructure for tourism should be built on any forest area in the islands. Tourist

activities in forest areas should be restricted to tented
accommodation or temporary wooden/prefabricated
structures that can be dismantled easily and moved to
another site. These areas should remain under the control
of the forest department which should be responsible for
ensuring that the quantum and type of tourism is such
that it does not in any way degrade the forests or other
ecosystems.

41) A proper eco-friendly tourism plan should be developed
for the islands within one year. This plan should also do
an economic and a distributional analysis to highlight
how tourism can make a net contribution to the economy
of the islands and how the economic benefits can be
equitably distributed among the various segments of the
local society and generate local employment.

42) Such a plan must be in conformity with the requirement
for conserving the ecological and cultural integrity of the
islands and not pose a security threat to this strategically
important area.

Miscellaneous Recommendations

43) The forest department and the administration of ANI
should make public at the beginning of each year the
proposed uses of natural resources, including forests.
This detailed information specifying, among other things,
uses, locations, quantum, purpose and users, and giving
details of the basis on which these decisions have been
made, should be published in the local newspapers and
also made available on a website to be maintained for
the purpose by the administration. At the end of each

year, actual use, deviations from the proposals and the reasons thereof must also be similarly made public.

44) The various forest working plans/protected area management plans should also be made accessible to the public, as soon as they are approved. Copies should be kept at all public libraries and other accessible places in the islands. In addition, copies should be freely made available to the general public, on demand, after charging actual costs of photocopying.

45) All officers of the administration, including forest officers, should undergo an orientation training of at least five days, every three years, to acquaint themselves with the ecological characteristics of the islands and the options available for their economic development in an environmentally and socially sustainable manner. Officers being posted from the mainland to these islands should be so oriented within three months of their posting.

46) The Government of India and the ANI Administration should consider setting up an Island Development Institute in ANI that can become a centre of research, training and education for managing island and coastal ecosystems in a sustainable manner. This institute could not only cater to national needs but, over time, also become a regional institution. A proposal to the effect already exists and was submitted to the IDA many years back. It can be suitably modified and considered.

47) There are many areas that need to be properly researched and many problems that need innovative solutions. These include:

- An assessment of the ecological differences between

worked and un-worked forests.
- Methods of returning the worked and encroached forests to their natural state.
- Methods of further working forests in a manner that minimizes impact on biodiversity and the environment.
- Methods to conserve soil and water.
- Feasibility of generating energy through non-conventional methods, including wind and tidal energy.
- Methods of treating garbage and other pollutants, thereby protecting the coastal and marine environment from degradation.
- Methods of using alternate building materials that are environmentally friendly and sustainable.

These and other required studies should be commissioned on a priority basis so that their findings can be urgently applied for the betterment of the islands.

Some possible implications of the recommendations

1) There is likely to be some loss of employment, as detailed below, if these recommendations were followed.
   a. Loss of about 300 jobs if Kitply Industries closes down as a result of these recommendations.
   b. Loss of about 2,000 jobs if the Andaman and Nicobar Islands Forest and Plantation Development Corporation closes down.
   c. Loss of some employment (exact quantum not

known) due to the ban on export of timber. However, this is likely to be very small, as very little timber was being sent to the mainland by private sawmills. In 1998-99 it was 923 cu. m., in 1999-2000 it was 570 cu. m. and in 2000-01 it was 614 cu. m.

   d. Surplus staff in the forest department due to curtailing of forest working and extraction.

   e. Some loss of livelihood due to the banning of extraction of sand.

   f. Some loss of road transport-related employment due to the banning of traffic on the ATR.

   g. Need for additional sources of livelihood for about 2,300 post-1978 forest encroachers, once they are removed from the forests.

2) However, following from these recommendations, there will also be significant cost-saving and additional employment opportunities, as detailed below.

   a. Savings on transport subsidies to the forest-based industry to the tune of five to six crore rupees per year.

   b. Savings from the closing down of two forest depots, one in Chennai and one in Kolkata, reportedly around one crore rupees a year.

   c. Additional employment for setting up forest protection forces.

   d. Additional employment in regenerating encroached areas and earlier worked forests.

   e. Additional employment in the shipping sector due to increased ferry traffic after closing down the ATR.

3) There are other relatively untapped or under-utilized areas of employment that can be developed. Including:

a. Fisheries – especially coastal – with local involvement. Current estimates suggest that only a small proportion of the fishery potential is being tapped. The islands have a continental shelf of 16,000 to 35,000 sq. km. (according to different sources) and an Exclusive Economic Zone (EEZ) of 600,000 sq. km., which is 28 per cent of the total Indian EEZ. The total potential has been variously calculated to be between 12,000 and 160,000 tonnes of fish per year (Master Plan for Andaman and Nicobar Islands for the Development of Fisheries, Government of India, Ministry of Agriculture, 1989), just from the shelf area. However, more recent estimates indicate between 45,000 and 160,000 tonnes per year. According to the ANI administration, the current levels of harvest are just a fraction of the harvestable potential (Volume II, page 136).

b. Production of goods/food for local use, and the consequent removal of subsidies for transportation of these goods from the mainland. At present, almost all the goods for local consumption come from the mainland. Their transportation, by ship, also costs the government dearly in subsidies. However, many of these goods can be produced locally. This would not only promote local employment and save on subsidies, but also cut down on the requirement for cargo space.

c. Handicrafts. There is great potential for developing the artisanal handicrafts industry and this could provide significant additional employment.

d. Swiftlet nest cultivation. This is potentially a very lucrative activity. There is great demand for swiftlet nests in the nearby south-east Asian countries, and 1 kg fetches between one and two lakh rupees. A note describing the potential has been enclosed in Volume II, page 300.

e. Orchid cultivation. This, again, has tremendous potential, as these islands have a large number of very beautiful and rare orchids.

f. Spices/medicinal plants, without expanding agricultural land. All official settlers in the islands were given two hectares of flat (valley) land and two hectares of hill land. Much of this hill land is still forested and its conversion to agricultural land, apart from not being economically viable, would also cause significant soil erosion and disrupt the water cycles. Therefore, this land can be used for activities conducive to soil and water conservation, like high value spices/medicinal plants. There are many valuable spices and medicinal plants that are found in the islands.

g. Eco-tourism. This, again, has tremendous potential. High-value specialized ecological tourism can generate a fair amount of local employment at all levels.

h. Water and soil conservation works. These are desperately needed in the ANI, which has acute water shortage and is also losing a lot of its topsoil, thereby disrupting the terrestrial, coastal and marine ecosystem. Existing schemes of the Government of India, like the watershed programme, can be extended and strengthened in these islands to both conserve the environment and generate employment.

4) Consequently, the potential for additional employment, if properly developed, is enough to offset any adverse impacts of the recommendations. Besides, if the islands are developed as a centre of education, research and training in island and coastal management, as recommended earlier, many additional jobs can be created. In fact, over time, caution will have to be exercised to ensure that the requirement for human power in the islands does not exceed the local supply, necessitating further migration from the mainland.

5) There is also some concern expressed by the ANI Forest Department that if felling in unworked forests was banned, then the worked forests and plantations would not be able to support even the local demands for timber. However, detailed discussions with the department and a scrutiny of documents and data bring out the following facts:

   a. The total area of worked forests in the Andamans, excluding Little Andaman, is approximately 100,000 ha.

   b. Most of these forests were worked in a manner such that only a proportion of the mature trees of commercial species were extracted and the immature ones left.

   c. Therefore, in each hectare of the worked forests there should now be a large number of mature trees that were either left behind as mother trees or that were immature when the logging was done fifty to sixty years ago, but are now mature and ready for harvesting.

d. As the surplus number of commercial trees, in excess of what would have been their numbers in a natural forest, have to be removed in order to allow the forests to return to as close a natural form as possible, the extraction of these mature trees would serve the dual purpose of providing timber for local consumption and returning the forests to a near-natural profile.

e. It has been estimated that at least 10 cu. m. per hectare can be safely and sustainably extracted from these worked forests, though once working plans are made, the figure might go up. Therefore, given that the total available worked forest is 100,000 ha, the total availability of commercial timber would work out to 1,000,000 cu. m. This would be enough to meet the local timber demands (calculated at 30,000 cu. m. per year currently, but likely to go down once timber conservation efforts are put in place) for at least thirty years, by which time additional timber would have become mature and harvestable.

f. In addition. There are over 12,500 ha of plantations of hardwoods done in the islands (annex 4). It is estimated that these plantations, that in any case need to be cleared so that the land can be regenerated, will provide 300 to 500 cu. m. per hectare, depending on the species. This would work out to between 37,50,000 to 62,50,000 cu. m. of timber, which would by itself be enough to meet the local hardwood requirements (calculated to be about 25,000 cu. m. per annum; for details, see Volume II, page 154-55, 161) for between 150 and 250 years. Needless to say, both in the plantations and in the worked forest areas, extraction should start first in the earliest plots and proceed to newer ones so that adequate time is given for regeneration.

6) The forest department has also expressed a concern that if no export of timber is allowed to the mainland, then this might lead to the artificial manipulation of timber prices locally and prices would be artificially forced down, as the forest department would have no option but to sell their timber locally or have it perish. However, considering that the forest department sawmills have a combined capacity of 29,000 cu. m. per year, they could, if required, process all the timber that is harvested in a year, thereby preventing it from deteriorating. Besides, once the capacity to treat timber has been enhanced, as recommended, there should be no danger of any timber being wasted if the local sawmills do not pick it up. In case, if timber in any month is not picked up, felling for subsequent months or seasons could be trimmed to take this into consideration.

7) A concern has also been expressed that forests need to be worked in case they are to remain healthy and that 'over-mature' and dead trees need to be removed. There is also the view that once a tree reaches a certain age, it has a 'negative increment' and, therefore, must be cut. However, these arguments do not stand up to scientific scrutiny. Forests have existed and continue to exist in areas where they have never been 'managed' by human beings. There are many examples of this in the Andaman and Nicobar Islands itself. The concern for negative increment and for 'healthy' forests is a concern that might be relevant to commercial plantations but is certainly

not tenable where natural forests are concerned. In fact, dead trees are as important a part of natural ecosystems, both as habitat to specialized species of fauna and flora and an input into the soil, as are live trees.

APPENDIX II

SUPREME COURT ORDER,
7 MAY 2002

IA No 502 in W.P. (C) No 202 of 1995
T.N. Godavarman Thirumalpad (Petitioner) Vs Union of
India & Ors. (Respondents)
(for intervention). Date: 7 May 2002

CORAM:

HON'BLE THE CHIEF JUSTICE
HON'BLE MR JUSTICE ARIJIT PASAYAT
HON'BLE MR JUSTICE H.K. SEMA

Upon hearing counsel, the Court made the following order:
    After hearing the learned Amicus Curiae, counsel for
the parties, and taking into consideration the affidavit of
the Union of India – Ministry of Environment and Forests
in relation to survey of [the] ecosystem of Andaman and
Nicobar Islands, the learned Amicus Curiae has made certain
suggestions. There does not seem to be any objection to this
Court in accepting the report of Shri Shekhar Singh that

some modifications have been suggested. We, therefore, in the first instance, accept the report of Shri Shekhar Singh.

On a query being raised by us, Mr Altaf Ahmed, learned Additional Solicitor General, appearing for The Union Territory of Andaman and Nicobar Islands on instructions informed the Court that there is no social forestry in Andaman and Nicobar Islands. The wood is being cut is from the natural forest and plantation of teak, etc. [and this] has taken place in the forest which had been worked, approximating 40,000 cubic metres of wood is cut from the forest annually for the purposes of the small mills, the total logging of wood being approximately 130,000 cubic metres per year. In the last two years, this figure has come down, but the fact remains that instead of resorting to social forestry and thereby providing employment to the people in growing forest at the present moment, the natural forests are being cut and the timber sawn.

Andaman and Nicobar Islands is one of the hot spots and is in the eco-fragile area and the eco-diversity thereby has to be preserved. For this, it is essential that the natural forest is protected and re-generation allowed to take place.

We are also informed that the existing sawmills have a subsisting licence valid till 30 March 2003. The sawmills and other wood-based industries in the Andaman and Nicobar Islands are not permitted to cut the trees and supplies to them are made only by the Government itself or through its Corporation. Some of these sawmills and industries have logs of wood and sawn timber in their stock. It would therefore be iniquitous to deprive them of an opportunity to utilize the stock for which payment has been made to the Government for the purchase of wood. However, it is to be borne in mind that fresh logging of wood must cease immediately.

After taking all facts and circumstances into consideration, we issue the following directions:

1) All felling of trees from the forest of Little Andaman Islands, the national park and sanctuaries, the tribal reserves and all other areas shall stand suspended.

2) For the areas in which there are working plans, the Government through the Chief Secretary shall disclose on an affidavit:

   i) The extent of felling and regeneration permitted under these working plans during the last ten years.

   ii) The compliance with regeneration/replantation/reforestation targets under the working plans and reasons if any for the shortfall.

3) The working plan of the Andaman and Nicobar Islands should be reworked on the basis as was applied to the State of MP and others, namely that before any felling of trees, there should first be compulsory afforestation/regeneration, the felling permissions would be based upon the extent of regeneration of forest undertaken and not the other way round.

4) No felling of tree (under the working plan or otherwise) shall be permitted for meeting any raw material requirements of the plywood, veneer, block board, match stick or any other wood-based industry.

5) In drawing up the new working plans, the Government shall formulate a Committee with one Ecologist who is proficient with the ecology of [the] Andamans.

6) The working plans so formulated shall be placed before this Court within a period of twelve weeks.

7) The trees felled under the working plan in the

manner indicated aforesaid should be utilized for the requirements of the local inhabitants.

8) The licences of all the sawmills and wood-based industries shall not be renewed after 31 March 2003. This will not debar the authorities from cancelling licences in accordance with law, if there is no breach of the Licence Committee by the licencees before that date.

9) The ecology of the area does not permit any kind of industrial activity for which the wood is likely to be consumed. Therefore, licences of wood-based industries shall stand cancelled but they will be permitted to exhaust the existing stock till 31 March 2003.

10) The Union of India, if it so adopts and thinks appropriate, may take steps for relocating the dislocated wood-based industries in the mainland area anywhere in India as long as it is not within the vicinity of forest area. Henceforth, for meeting the local requirements, it is only the Government sawmills which shall operate. No fresh wood or logs shall be given to any of the sawmills or wood-based industries till fresh working plans are prepared and submitted to this Court and the approval obtained.

11) With immediate effect, there will be no movement of logs or timber in any form including sawn timber from Andaman and Nicobar Islands to any part of India or anywhere else.

12) Regularization of encroachments on forestland in any form, including allotment/use of forestland for agricultural or horticultural purposes, shall be strictly prohibited.

13) All those families who have been identified as having

encroached on forestland prior to 1978 and have not yet shifted to their allotted rehabilitation sites shall be given one month's notice to vacate their encroachments and shift to the allotted land. Failing this, their allotment shall be cancelled and they shall be forcibly evicted within three months of the deadline being over, without any further claim to land or any other form of rehabilitation. Such notices should be issued within six weeks.

14) Similarly, those among the pre-1978 families who have shifted to their allotted sites but have occupied more land than they were entitled to shall also be given one month's notice to vacate the extra land occupied by them. On the expiry of this notice period, the allotments of those who have not complied with this notice shall be cancelled and they should be forcibly evicted within three months, without any further claim to compensation or land. Such notices should be issued within six weeks.

15) All post-1978 forest encroachments shall be completely removed within three months.

16) For the eviction of encroachers, an effective action plan shall be prepared and implemented under direct supervision, monitoring and control of a Committee under the Chairmanship of the Lt Governor with Chief Secretary, Principal Chief Conservator of Forests and reputed NGO representatives, its members. The Chief Secretary, Andaman and Nicobar Islands, shall file every month an affidavit about progress of eviction of encroachments.

17) The process of issue of identity cards to all the residents shall be completed within a period of six months.

18) The extraction of sand shall be phased out at minimum

20 per cent per year on reducing balance basis to bring the sand mining to the level of 33 per cent of the present level of mining within a maximum period of five years.

19) The approvals accorded by Ministry of Environment and Forests under the Forest (Conservation) Act, 1980, shall be reviewed by a Committee consisting of Secretary, Environment and Forests, Director General of Forests and at least one non-official member of the Forest Advisory Committee constituted under the Forest (Conservation) Rules to restrict the approvals to the barest minimum needed to serve emergent public purposes. Felling of trees shall commence only after the process of compensatory afforestation has actually been undertaken on the ground. In future, proposals shall be considered for approval only after detailed Environmental Impact Assessment has been carried out through an independent agency identified by Ministry of Environment and Forests.

20) Specific actions shall be undertaken by Ministry of Environment and Forests/Andaman and Nicobar Islands Administration on the other recommendations of Shri Shekhar Singh Report which are not specifically dealt with in above orders. Ministry of Environment and forests and the Andaman and Nicobar Islands Administration shall file an affidavit within three months giving details of action taken by them on each of such recommendations.

Copy of this order be sent by the Registry to the Chief Secretary, Andaman and Nicobar Islands for information and compliance.

APPENDIX III

POLICY ON THE JARAWA TRIBE OF ANDAMAN ISLANDS*

I. Introduction

The High Court of Calcutta (Circuit Bench at Port Blair) vide their order dated 9 April 2001 in WP No 048 of 1999 (PIL) – Ms Shyamali Ganguly, Advocate Vs Union of India and Others; inter alia, directed the Central Government as under:

'The Central Government through the Principal Secretary, Ministry of Home Affairs, within two months from the communication of this order shall form a Committee of Experts with the Lt Governor of the Islands as the Convener, comprising renowned Anthropologists, Sociologists, Nutrition Experts, Doctors for immediately undertaking a scientific study, research and survey in the aforesaid change in the behaviour of the Jarawas and to find out the cause of the same ...

The said Committee shall submit its report within six months from the formation of such Committee before

---

* As approved by the Calcutta High Court

235

the Central Government and Lt Governor, Andaman and Nicobar Islands and also shall file a copy thereof before the Circuit Bench of this Court.

Within six months thereafter, the Central Government through the Home Secretary himself and the Lt Governor of the Andaman and Nicobar Administration shall formulate a policy, plans and programmes on the aforesaid questions whether the steps should now be taken for bringing the Jarawas into the mainstream of the society or they should be left to their own way of life as before or a balance between the two should be struck following the peaceful existence theory as suggested by Mr Awaradi in his Master Plan or any other experts. For the aforesaid purpose, the Central Government shall arrange seminars and open discussions of the different experts, national and international on the line, Anthropologist, Sociologist and others as also individuals and non-governmental organizations having knowledge and experience in the matter, inviting them by issuing public notification in widely circulated newspapers and sending them letters of invitation and thereafter shall frame the policy decision within the stipulated period after deliberation and discussion on such opinions with the approval of the concerned Ministry. The Central Government shall also publish the papers, discussions and deliberation of such seminar, at its cost, for future reference …

After formulation of such policy, the same shall be notified by the Central Government and the A&N Administration and shall also be placed before the Circuit Bench of this Hon'ble Court for appropriate order.'

2. In pursuance of the aforesaid order of the Hon'ble High Court of Calcutta, a Committee of Experts was constituted

by the Central Government vide the Ministry of Home Affairs' Notification No U-14040/24/99-ANI dated 21 July 2001.

3. The Committee of Experts submitted its report before the Hon'ble High Court of Calcutta on 28 July 2003. As per the aforesaid directions of the Hon'ble High Court, the Central Government was required to formulate policy, plans and programmes in respect of Jarawas in consultation with the Lt Governor, A&N Islands, after organizing seminars and open discussions with the different experts, national and international, Anthropologists, Sociologists and others as also individuals and non-governmental organizations having knowledge and experience in the matter. Accordingly, the Central Government organized two such seminars, one at Kolkata on 7–8 April 2004 and another at Port Blair on 27–28 May 2004 wherein experts, non-governmental organizations and individuals deliberated on various issues relating to the Jarawas and their well-being.

4. The Central Government in the Ministry of Home Affairs considered the report of Committee of Experts vis-à-vis the views that emerged during the two seminars/open discussions organized by the Central Government on the said report of the Expert Committee in consultation with the A&N Administration and the Ministry of Tribal Affairs, the administrative Ministry for the matters connected with tribes and tribal affairs.

5. The Central Government in the Ministry of Home Affairs has consequently decided to frame a policy/guidelines for the protection and welfare of the Jarawas in Andaman and Nicobar Islands with the following objectives in view.

II. Objectives

i) To protect the Jarawas from harmful effects of exposure and contact with the outside world while they are not physically, socially and culturally prepared for such interface;

ii) To preserve the social organization, mode of subsistence and cultural identity of the Jarawa community;

iii) To provide medical help to the Jarawas to reduce mortality and morbidity in case of their sudden affliction with diseases which their systems are unaccustomed to;

iv) To conserve the ecology and environment of the Jarawa Reserve Territory and strengthen support systems in order to enable the Jarawas [to] pursue their traditional modes of subsistence and way of life; and

v) To sensitize settler communities around the Jarawas' habitat and personnel working for the protection and preservation of the Jarawas about the need to preserve this ancient community and to value their unique culture and life styles.

III. Strategies/guidelines

The Central Government, with the above objectives in view, has framed the following strategies/guidelines for the protection and welfare of the Jarawas:

1. Protection of cultural identity

a) The Jarawas shall be considered and treated as a unique human heritage.

b) A policy of maximum autonomy to the Jarawas with minimum and regulated intervention shall be adopted by the Government towards the Jarawas. There shall be no intervention in cultural life of the Jarawas and they will be left at liberty to develop according to their own genius and at their own pace. No attempts to bring them into the mainstream society against their conscious will or to rehabilitate them in separate islands/locations at this stage of their social development will be made.

c) The quality of intervention with Jarawas will be managed with care and sensitivity through suitably trained and reoriented personnel, in consultation with and evaluation by anthropologists and experts. The objective will be to avoid dependency syndrome and to ensure their development as a vibrant social group. The personnel working for Jarawas would be provided with proper training and sensitization. The people of the villages near the Jarawa reserve area and other non-tribals will be sensitized regarding the rights and privileges of the Jarawas.

2. Protection of the Natural Habitat

a) No exploitation of natural resources within the Jarawa reserve by any non-tribal including Government agencies will be allowed. Necessary measures shall be initiated to curb even occasional extraction of resources from the Jarawa territory by non-Jarawas. Provisions of A&N Islands (Protection of Aboriginal Tribes) Regulation, 1956, will be enforced more effectively. The A&N Islands (Protection of Aboriginal Tribes) Regulation, 1956, shall be amended to provide stringent punishment for poaching in the Jarawa territory and for exploitation of the Jarawas.

b) The notified Jarawa territory shall be fully and effectively demarcated and no attempt to curtail, reduce or to acquire land therefrom shall be made.

c) All encroachments in the Jarawa territory shall be removed on priority basis. Stringent arrangements to ensure that such encroachments do not take place in future will also be made.

d) Permanent residence of Government employees/non-tribals in the Jarawa reserve will not be allowed.

e) It shall be ensured that no person other than a Jarawa is allowed to enter the notified Jarawa reserve by any means unless he/she is permitted by the competent authority designated by the A&N Administration for this purpose. However, no such permission shall be granted unless the person is proceeding on bonafide work relating to the welfare of the Jarawas or protection of the area.

f) No tourist will be allowed to visit/interact with the Jarawas so that curious intrusions are avoided as these intrusions adversely affect their lifestyle and health.

3. Protection of Health Status

a) Periodic health survey of the Jarawa community will be organized through a Standing Team of health professionals. Only cases needing intensive care will be brought to the hospital but they will be kept in separate enclosures. Appropriate food will be provided instead of the hospital meals. Whenever female Jarawas come or are brought to hospital, female Police will be posted invariably.

b) Medical intervention among the Jarawas, i.e., the line of treatment, use of drugs and medicines will be only on the basis of advice of experts in the relevant fields and shall be administered only when found absolutely necessary.

c) Medical assistance to Jarawas will be extended in their reserve area by qualified health officials as far as feasible so that all the advantages of such in-situ treatment are available to the Jarawas. Jarawa patients will be shifted to hospital only if in-situ treatment is not possible or not felt adequate to save the patient.

d) The traditional knowledge of Jarawas including ethnomedicine shall be preserved and documented.

e) Diagnostic approach, treatment regimen and prescription of drugs in case of common pattern of diseases observed amongst the Jarawas shall be standardized and documented so that experimentation by individual doctors and conflicting assessments can be avoided.

f) Periodic nutritional and food security surveys shall be conducted to ensure that there is adequate provision of food resources to the Jarawas and that there is no fall in nutritional standards.

g) The Jarawas shall not be provided food which is alien to their normal dietary habits.

h) Officials/workers engaged in the protection and welfare of Jarawas will be regularly screened to ensure that they are absolutely free from any communicable diseases and that they do not encourage addictive habits such as smoking and drinking amongst the Jarawa population.

4. Regulation of traffic on Andaman Trunk Road

a) Traffic on Andaman Trunk Road will be regulated strictly limiting the traffic to the essential purposes of public transport, supplies and emergency evacuation of patients and to ensure that it is an innocent and harmless passage and not a source of trouble to Jarawas.

b) Vehicles on Andaman Trunk Road will be allowed to move only in restricted hours and in convoy under notified speed limit to avert possible road accidents and to avoid any sort of interaction of travellers with Jarawas.

c) Facilities for travel by boat/ship will be strengthened and transportation/travel by sea will be encouraged.

d) Maintenance of the Andaman Trunk Road will be carried out by a mobile maintenance team bringing men, machine and materials from Ferrargunj/Jirkatang and carrying out the job only during daytime.

e) The tourist traffic on Andaman Trunk Road will be strictly monitored to ensure that there is no interaction between the Jarawas and the tourists.

5. Codification of Jarawa language

a) Codification of the language of Jarawas shall be done with the advice and involvement of experts. However, continuous interaction in the name of codification of language will not be allowed. Codification of language shall be attempted by relevant experts in a discreet manner during periodic health surveys of the Jarawas

b) Officials of the A&N Administration who will be coming in contact with the Jarawas, particularly those of Health and Welfare Departments, will be encouraged to learn the Jarawa language so that they are able to communicate with them and understand their perceptions, reactions and problems.

6. Institutional arrangements

a) The A&N Administration shall be wholly and entirely responsible for the implementation of the aforesaid policy on the Jarawas. It shall lay down detailed tasks for each agency and unit of the administrative machinery and set up structures for monitoring and specific mechanism for enforcing accountability of officials in respect of tasks assigned to them in connection with protection and welfare of the Jarawas.

b) The Andaman Adim Janjati Vikas Samiti (AAJVS), an autonomous body, will function like a trustee of the interest of the Jarawas and advise A&N Administration regarding the protection and welfare of all aboriginal tribes including the Jarawas.

c) The Executive Council of AAJVS assisted by experts and persons having knowledge and experience in tribal affairs under the Chairmanship of Lt Governor will enforce and monitor implementation of the policy.

d) Meaningful research on the Jarawas will be allowed under the advice of AAJVS to further the understanding of their life and culture, including their traditional knowledge. However, it shall be ensured strictly that the confidentiality of genetic resources on the Jarawas will be maintained and not used for commercial exploitation by any agency or organization which is not directly concerned with the welfare and protection of the Jarawas.

e) Periodic review of this policy will done so that the policy is dynamic and takes into account changing needs and circumstances.

APPENDIX IV

POWER TO THE NATIVE

By Zubair Ahmed[1]

Indian Express, 3 April 2016

There are two thousand square miles of country teeming with food for the Jarawas and unoccupied by any human being. Why must they keep coming over to our hundred-square mile settlements and keep killing our wretched convicts?

– Lt Col. Michael Lloyd Ferrar
Chief Commissioner (1921–33), Andaman Islands,
writing in March 1926

The advent of the British colonialists in 1858 to set up a penal settlement in Andaman Islands posed a challenge to the tribals inhabiting the islands. The Jarawas resisted attempts to colonize their land and lives. Even after Independence,

---

[1] Zubair Ahmed is a Port Blair–based writer and researcher and editor of weekly news magazine *The Light of Andamans*.

Jarawas were seen as a threat to settlers. To keep the tribe at bay, bush police forces were engaged until the Jarawas themselves realized their vulnerability, shed hostilities, and came out of the forests in 1998. The hand of friendship they extended towards the outside world has proved to be disastrous for the tribe, who lived in the forest for the last 50,000 years or more and now number around 400.

A policy of 'isolation with minimal intervention' was brought into force in 2004, an important contemporary watershed. With the passage of time, and ineffective implementation of the policy, the Jarawas remain caught between two worlds – and secure in neither.

While the murder of a Jarawa child by a fellow tribesman in Tirur and the associated legal conundrum is making headlines worldwide, one pertinent question not being dealt with is the ongoing sexual exploitation of the Jarawa women by outsiders. It obscures the fact that first, a crime has been committed by someone who breached the reserve and sexually exploited a Jarawa woman.

In all these years, the state has failed in securing the reserve against poachers, who exploit the tribe as well as prey on forest resources. More unfortunate has been the inability to sensitize the settlers living along the fringes of the Jarawa Tribal Reserve and even the islanders about the rich 'human heritage' and the particular vulnerabilities of the Jarawa community. This has been an opportunity missed to rope in the large settler population of the islands as the protectors or at least well-wishers of the tribe.

In contrast, the level of illicit contact has increased manifold in all three sectors – Middle Strait and Kadamtala in Middle Andaman and Tirur in South Andaman – where several cases of sexual exploitation of women have been reported. With poachers becoming the contact points for the Jarawas, alcohol and drugs have made inroads into the reserve. Several poachers have been charged with luring the Jarawas with alcohol and food to part with forest produce.

The changed realities and the bad press the Andaman and Nicobar administration got from across the world, particularly after a video of Jarawas dancing for tourists in lieu of food surfaced in 2012, did force a relook into the policy. A committee of experts set up in 2011 went on to make the rules, regulations and laws governing the tribal reserve more stringent to ward off 'undesirable' elements. An overenthusiastic administration tied itself up in knots in creating an unrealistic 5-km. buffer zone for the tribal reserve. It turned the settlers firmly against the administration and also the Jarawa community.

The appointment of anthropologist Vishvajit Pandya as the director of the Port Blair–based Andaman and Nicobar Tribal Research Institute (ANTRI) in 2013 was a significant one. Pandya not only convinced the reluctant and overcautious administration of the islands to look beyond the existing policy framework, but he also played an important role in bringing drastic changes in the tribal welfare agency, the Andaman Adim Janjati Vikas Samiti (AAJVS), and in empowering and reorienting the grass-roots workers who deal with the Jarawas on a daily basis.

Earlier, the trained social workers of AAJVS, fairly competent in special tribal languages, were only meant to do the bidding of bureaucrats. Under Pandya, they went back to listening to the Jarawas and implementing policies with their informed consent. For instance, though the Jarawas preferred to be in their 'traditional attire', when they are assisted by the AAJVS to move from one place to other by jeep or boat, they are keen to cover their body. It is, perhaps, a way of resisting the tourist experience and expectation of the Jarawa as a 'naked exotic' people.

An educational project, ang-katha, was also implemented inside the tribal reserve for Jarawa children, primarily aiming to prepare them for a bicultural future, where a Jarawa child could operate in the 'mainstream' but also be able to retain her own identity with pride and dignity.

Two additional points also need to be made here. The first is about the Indian media, which in the case of the islands and the Jarawas, always seems to be taking a cue from what the foreign media publishes. It needs to play a far more proactive role, including that of a watchdog. The second is the lacuna in the local education system where there is little, if anything, about the local geography and history of the indigenous people. When what is proximate is made so alien from the very beginning, a long-term and meaningful resolution is not going to be easy to come by.

Looking at the current incident in a larger context will also help to identify that which is more important and relevant. We have miserably failed in dealing with the honour killings by khap panchayats of Haryana and the Dalit killings in Tamil Nadu despite a whole gambit of laws and constitutional protection. So, instead of discussing the honour killing by a Jarawa, a tribe that occupies a very special position due to its geographical, historical, cultural and social condition, the focus should be on a policy framework, where the Jarawas are protected from the evils of 'civilization' and are allowed the time and space to decide their own future.

ANDAMAN AND NICOBAR ISLANDS: A HISTORICAL TIMELINE

1789: British East India Company decides to set up colony in the Andaman Islands; Lt Hyde Colebrooke visits the islands, meets native islanders and records some of their language. It is found out later that it belongs to the Jarawa; the colony that was set up was abandoned a few years later.

1839: Earliest known exploration of flora of the Andamans by Russian scientist Hefler; he lost his life to the hostility of the local inhabitants.

1857: Sepoy mutiny, also known as the first war of Indian independence.

1858: Establishment of the penal settlement in the Andamans by the British.

1860: A track cut from Port Blair in the east to Port Mouat in the west by the British; Jarawas were occasionally met in peaceful interactions and reportedly took away some useful metal articles

1863:   First reported attack on the British by the Jarawa; Rev. Corbyn undertakes an expedition to the Jarawa area.

1867:   Attack by the Onge on the British ship *Assam Valley*.

1869:   One of the first records/accounts of timber extraction from the Andaman forests.

1873:   First record of syphilis among the indigenous peoples of the islands.

1875:   First record of deaths in conflict with the Jarawas; six convicts and two Jarawas killed.

1878:   One Jarawa woman and two children captured during an expedition near Constance Bay.

1880:   Jarawas kill an Andamanese man at Port Campbell; Little Andaman is visited by British officer M.V. Portman.

1886:   Epidemic of measles in the Andaman forests.

1890s: Onges of Little Andaman Island contacted through gift-giving expeditions by the British; also believed to be the time when the Jarawas first started occupying Middle Andaman Island.

1891:   Jarawas first occupy parts of Baratang Island.

1896:   Construction work of the Cellular Jail starts.

1901:   First census in the islands. Total population of the Andaman Islands: 18,138; Jarawa population estimate: 585; Onge estimate: 672; Sentinelese estimate: 117; Great Andamanese actual count: 625; the Aka-Bea-Da, one of the ten groups constituting the Great Andamanese community goes extinct.

1902:   Punitive expedition against the Jarawa by the British.

1906:   First Working Plan for the forests prepared by
            F.H. Todd; construction work of Cellular Jail
            completed.

1911:   Jarawa population estimate: 114; Onge
            estimate: 631; Sentinelese estimate: 117; Great
            Andamanese actual count: 455; Total population
            of the Andaman Islands: 17,641.

1921:   Jarawa population estimate: 114; Onge
            estimate: 346; Sentinelese estimate: 117; Great
            Andamanese actual count: 209; Total population
            of the Andaman Islands: 17,814; clear felling
            system for extraction of timber introduced in the
            Andaman forests.

1925:   Establishment of the Karen village of Webi on
            Middle Andaman Island; the Moplahs were also
            settled in the Andamans around this time.

1931:   Jarawa population estimate: 70; Onge estimate:
            250; Sentinelese estimate: 50; Great Andamanese
            actual count: 90; Total population of the
            Andaman Islands: 19,223.

1941:   Total population of the Andaman Islands: 21,316

1942:   Occupation of the Andaman Islands by the
            Japanese.

1947:   India's Independence.

1950s: Remnants of Great Andamanese community
            (estimated to be a total of nineteen individuals)
            settled on Strait Island.

1951:   Jarawa population estimate: 50; Onge estimate:
            150; Sentinelese estimate: 50; Great Andamanese
            actual count: 23. Total population of the
            Andaman Islands: 18,962; Little Andaman is

visited by Italian anthropologist Cipriani to study the Onges.

1952: Chengappa's Working Plan for the Andaman forests.

1956: Notification of the Andaman and Nicobar Protection of Aboriginal Tribes Regulation (ANPATR) by the Government of India.

1957: Creation of tribal reserves in the names of the Jarawa, Onge and Sentinelese communities under the provision of the ANPATR; the Nicobar islands are also declared a tribal reserve; bush police outpost set up at Louis Islet.

1961: Jarawa population estimate: 500; Onge actual count: 129; Sentinelese estimate: 50; Great Andamanese actual count: 19; Total population of the Andaman Islands: 48,985.

1965: Report by the 'The Inter-Departmental Team on Accelerated Development Programme for the A&N islands', Ministry of Rehabilitation, Government of India.

1969: 366 East Pakistan families settled in Little Andaman.

1970: Survey for the establishment of red oil palm plantation on Little Andaman Island; first sawmill is set up on Little Andaman Island; annual intake 2,000 cu. m of timber.

1971: Jarawa population estimate: 250; Onge actual count: 112; Sentinelese estimate: 82; Great Andamanese actual count: 24. Total population of the Andaman Islands: 93,468.

1972:   First amendment to the Onge Tribal Reserve on Little Andaman Island.

1973:   165 Nicobari families settled in Harmander Bay area on Little Andaman Island. Forest Department (FD) assessment of timber productivity of the island's forests.

1974:   First contact mission by the A&N Administration to establish friendly contact with the Jarawas along the west coast of the Jarawa Tribal Reserve.

1975:   FD initiates work on the oil palm plantation in Little Andaman Island.

1975–76:   Creation of the first 160 ha of oil palm plantation.

1976:   Creation of the Andaman Adim Janjati Vikas Samiti (Andaman Tribal Welfare Society); presentation of Andaman and Nicobar Forest Plantation and Development Corporation (ANFPDC) proposal for logging and forestry operations in Little Andaman.

1977:   ANFPDC starts functioning; second amendment to the Onge Tribal Reserve; two Jarawa men, one with an old bullet wound, were brought to Port Blair and then returned to the forest in the hope that they would carry the message of trust and goodwill.

1977–79:   118 families from mainland settled on Little Andaman.

1979:   De-notification of parts of the Jarawa Tribal Reserve to facilitate timber extraction, construction of the Andaman Trunk Road and clearing of forests for settlements, horticulture and agriculture.

1981: Jarawa population estimate: 250; Onge actual count: 97; Sentinelese estimate: 100; Great Andamanese actual count: 26. Total population of the Andaman Islands: 158,287.

1983: Study of the Onge by anthropologist Vishvajit Pandya.

1988–89: Construction of the Andaman Trunk Road completed.

1990: Master Plan 1991–2021 for Welfare of Primitive Tribes of Andaman and Nicobar Islands by S.A. Awaradi.

1991: Jarawa population estimate: 280; Onge actual count: 95; Sentinelese estimate: 100; Great Andamanese actual count: 45. Total population of the Andaman Islands: 241,453; Jarawas attack the bush police camp at Jirkatang and kill one policeman; another amendment to the Onge Tribal Reserve, Little Andaman Island.

1992: Jarawas attack the bush police camp near Tirur

1996: 60–70 Jarawas surround timber extraction party at Puttatang, killing some labourers and injuring some; Supreme Court of India ruling related to forests in the Godavarman case, also called the 'Forest case'; patenting controversy related to Onge knowledge of medicinal plants.

1998: Petition filed by three NGOs in Calcutta High Court, Port Blair bench, regarding timber logging in the Onge Tribal Reserve on Little Andaman Island.

1999: Another petition filed by Port Blair–based lawyer in Calcutta High Court regarding the well-being and protection of the Jarawa tribal community; Measles epidemic amongst the Jarawas.

1998–99:   Jarawa hostility to the outside world comes to a gradual end.

2000:   Jarawa raid on the settlement of Sippi Tikry in North Andaman Island.

2001:   Jarawa actual count: 240; Onge actual count: 96; Sentinelese estimate: 39; Great Andamanese actual count: 43. Total population of the Andaman Islands: 314,239.

2002:   Supreme Court of India orders for the closure of the Andaman Trunk Road in those parts that run through the forests of the Jarawa Tribal Reserve

2004:   A 'Jarawa' Policy asking, mainly, for the Jarawa to be left alone is formulated in response to an order of Calcutta High Court seeking a policy related to the Jarawas; area of Jarawa Tribal Reserve re-notified and increased to about 1,000 sq. km.; earthquake off the Sumatra coast, followed by the tsunami.

2005:   Eruption of volcano on Barren Island.

2006:   Another outbreak of measles reported amongst the Jarawa; subgroup of experts on the Jarawa constituted by the Planning Commission submits its report. The group is chaired jointly by Dr Syeda Hameed, member, Planning Commission and Mr Jairam Ramesh, member, National Advisory Council.

2007:   A&N administration notifies a 5-km buffer zone around the Jarawa Tribal Reserve.

2010:   Boa Sr, the eighty-five-year-old woman believed
         to be the last speaker of the Bo language (in the
         Great Andamanese group) dies; expert committee
         formed to review Jarawa policy of 2004.

2011:   Jarawa actual count: 383; Great Andamanese
         actual count: 54. Total population of the
         Andaman Islands: 380,581.

2012:   A controversy breaks out as British newspaper
         Sunday Observer releases a short video showing
         six 'naked' Jarawa women dancing on the
         Andaman Trunk Road at the insistence of
         unseen male voices; A&N administration issues a
         modification diluting the buffer zone notification
         of 2007.

2013:   Amendment to the ANPATR; buffer zone
         modified again; Supreme Court of India orders
         closure of the Andaman Trunk Road for tourist
         traffic but allows for it to restart a few weeks
         later; establishment of the Andaman and Nicobar
         Tribal Research Institute.

INDEX

257

Local-Borns Association, 35
Logging of timber. *See* Timber

Madras Crocodile Bank Trust.
    See MCBT
Mangroves, xiii, 30, 100, 101,
    132, 135, 177
Mayabundar, 27, 214
MCBT, 98, 106
Measles, 249, also *see*
    epidemic
    outbreak in Jarawa
        community, xxvi, 6,
        40, 67–70, 74, 254
Megapode, Nicobari, 127,
    164, 183, 201
    habitat of the, 133, 164,
        166, 175, 193
    impact due to earthquake/
        tsunami, 133, 177, 201
    studies of the, 127, 177,
        201
    threat to, 133, 164, 166,
        177, 193, 201
Menchal Island, xxx
Meroe Island, xxx
    military activity on, 163,
        164
    tribal reserve, 169
Middle Andaman Island, xxx,
    24, 58, 69, 100, 116, 160,

192, 244, 250
    impact of earthquake/
        tsunami, 173
    Important Bird Area, 195
    Jarawas in, 24, 58, 59, 74,
        86, 245, 249 (also *see*
        Jarawas)
    JTR, 62, 195, 213
Migration
    mainlanders to the islands,
        xxv, also see Inner Line
        Area
Militaristic vision, xxvii, 165
Military/ militarization, 159
    catalysed by the tsunami,
        159
    conflict over land in
        Camorta, 164, 165
    infrastructure
        development, xix, xxiv
Mining
    beach sand, xxv, 72, 153
    impact on sea turtle
        nesting, 99, 100
    SC orders on beach sand
        mining, 34, 35, 36, 107,
        192, 217, 233
Ministry of Environment and
    Forests, xviii
Ministry of Road Transport,
    xix

The definitive Andaman novel

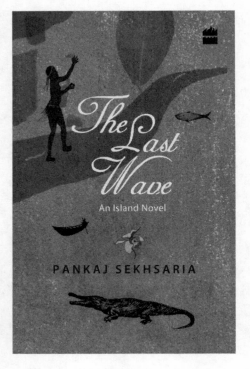

The Last Wave is a story of lost loves, but also of a culture, a community, an ecology poised on the sharp edge of time and history.

ISBN: 978-93-5136-191-6
Price: ₹350

Praise for *The Last Wave*

'*The Last Wave: An Island Novel* is fascinating for the way it depicts a part of India often ignored in literature.'

—*www.southasiabookblog.com*

'[A] poignant yet engaging tale of a group of tiny islands, which seldom find a worthy note of mention in "mainland India", save for tourism and administrative purposes. Unless you are an anthropologist or an anthropology student, you will hardly get to read a work of literature so soothingly immersed in that unusual milieu.'

—*The Financial Express*

'[A] commendable debut.'

—Ajay Dandekar in *Biblio*

📖 HarperCollins *Publishers* India

🐦 @HarperCollinsIN

📷 @HarperCollinsIN

📘 @HarperCollinsIN

🔗 HarperCollins Publishers India

www.harpercollins.co.in

Harper Broadcast

Showcasing celebrated authors, book reviews, plot trailers, cover reveals, launches and interviews, Harper Broadcast is live and available for free subscription on the brand's social media channels through a new newsletter. Hosted by renowned TV anchor and author Amrita Tripathi, Broadcast is a snapshot of all that is news, views, extracts, sneak peeks and opinions on books. Tune in to conversations with authors, where we get up close and personal about their books, why they write and what's coming up.

Harper Broadcast is the first of its kind in India, a publisher-hosted news channel for all things publishing within HarperCollins. Follow us on Twitter and YouTube.

Subscribe to the monthly newsletter here: https://harpercollins.co.in/newsletter/

📺 Harper Broadcast

🐦 @harperbroadcast

www.harperbroadcast.com

Address

HarperCollins *Publishers* India Ltd
A-75, Sector 57, Noida, UP 201301, India

Phone
+91 120-4044800

25 📖 HarperCollins India Ltd

Celebrating 25 Years of Great Publishing

HarperCollins India celebrates its twenty-fifth anniversary this year. Twenty-five years of publishing India's finest writers and some of its most memorable books – those you cannot put down; ones you want to finish reading yet don't want to end; works you can read over and over again only to fall deeper in love with.

Through the years, we have published writers from the Indian subcontinent, and across the globe, including Aravind Adiga, Kiran Nagarkar, Amitav Ghosh, Jhumpa Lahiri, Manu Joseph, Anuja Chauhan, Upamanyu Chatterjee, A.P.J. Abdul Kalam, Shekhar Gupta, M.J. Akbar, Satyajit Ray, Gulzar, Surender Mohan Pathak and Anita Nair, amongst others, with approximately 200 new books every year and an active print and digital catalogue of more than 1000 titles, across ten imprints. Publishing works of various genres including literary fiction, poetry, mind body spirit, commercial fiction, journalism, business, self-help, cinema, biographies – all with attention to quality, of the manuscript and the finished product – it comes as no surprise that we have won every major literary award including the Man Booker Prize, the Sahitya Akademi Award, the DSC Prize, the Hindu Literary Prize, the MAMI Award for Best Writing on Cinema, the National Award for Best Book on Cinema, the Crossword Book Award, and the Publisher of the Year, twice, at Publishing Next in Goa, and more recently, the Publisher of the Year Award 2016 at Tata Literature Live, Mumbai.

We credit our success to the people who make us who we are, and will be celebrating this anniversary with: our authors, retailers, partners, readers and colleagues at HarperCollins India. Over the years, a firm belief in our promise and our passion to deliver only the very best of the printed word has helped us become one of India's finest in publishing. Every day we endeavour to deliver bigger and better – for you.

Thank you for your continued support and patronage. And here's wishing everyone a great new year!